THE ULTIMATE GOLF TRIVIA CHALLENGE

OVER 600 QUIZ QUESTIONS
FOR DIE-HARD GOLF FANS

HANK PATTON

ISBN: 979-8-89095-055-0

Copyright © 2025 by Curious Press

ALL RIGHTS RESERVED

No part of this book may be reproduced, stored in a retrieval system, or transmitted in any form or by any means, electronic, mechanical, photocopying, recording, scanning, or otherwise, without the prior written permission of the publisher.

CONTENTS

INTRODUCTION 1

CHAPTER 1: GOLF'S EARLY HISTORY 2
   Chapter 1 Answers: 7
   Did You Know? 8

CHAPTER 2: Golf's Spread 9
   Chapter 2 Answers: 14
   Did You Know? 15

CHAPTER 3: The Early Open Championship Years 16
   Chapter 3 Answers: 21
   Did You Know? 22

CHAPTER 4: The Amateur Championship 23
   Chapter 4 Answers: 28
   Did You Know? 29

CHAPTER 5: THE 1890S 30
   Chapter 5 Answers: 35
   Did You Know? 36

CHAPTER 6: THE 1900S 37
   Chapter 6 Answers: 41
   Did You Know? 42

CHAPTER 7: THE 1910S 43
   Chapter 7 Answers: 47
   Did You Know? 48

CHAPTER 8: THE 1920S 49
   Chapter 8 Answers: 54
   Did You Know? 55

CHAPTER 9: THE 1930S 56
   Chapter 9 Answers: 60

Did You Know? 61

CHAPTER 10: THE 1940S **62**
    Chapter 10 Answers: 67
    Did You Know? 68

CHAPTER 11: THE 1950S **69**
    Chapter 11 Answers: 74
    Did You Know? 75

CHAPTER 12: THE 1960S **76**
    Chapter 12 Answers: 81
    Did You Know? 82

CHAPTER 13: THE 1970S **83**
    Chapter 13 Answers: 88
    Did You Know? 89

CHAPTER 14: THE 1980S **90**
    Chapter 14 Answers: 95
    Did You Know? 96

CHAPTER 15: THE 1990S **97**
    Chapter 15 Answers: 101
    Did You Know? 102

CHAPTER 16: THE 2000S **103**
    Chapter 16 Answers: 107
    Did You Know? 108

CHAPTER 17: THE 2010S **109**
    Chapter 17 Answers: 114
    Did You Know? 115

CHAPTER 18: 2020 TO 2024 .... **116**
    Chapter 18 Answers: 121
    Did You Know? 122

CHAPTER 19: The Professional Golfers' Association **123**

Chapter 19 Answers: 127

Did You Know? 128

CHAPTER 20: The Ladies Professional Golf Association 129

Chapter 20 Answers: 133

Did You Know? 134

CHAPTER 21: LIV GOLF 135

Chapter 21 Answers: 139

Did You Know? 140

CHAPTER 22: Senior Professional Golf 141

Chapter 22 Answers: 146

Did You Know? 147

CHAPTER 23: Major Champions 148

Chapter 23 Answers: 153

Did You Know? 154

CHAPTER 24: The Ryder Cup 155

Chapter 24 Answers: 160

Did You Know? 161

CHAPTER 25: Golf at the Olympics 162

Chapter 25 Answers: 167

Did You Know? 168

CHAPTER 26: The Old Course at St Andrews 169

Chapter 26 Answers: 174

Did You Know? 175

CHAPTER 27: Augusta National Golf Club 176

Chapter 27 Answers: 181

Did You Know? 182

CHAPTER 28: Shinnecock Hills Golf Club 183

Chapter 28 Answers: 188

Did You Know? 189

CHAPTER 29: Pebble Beach Golf Links 190
    Chapter 29 Answers: 195
    Did You Know? 196

CHAPTER 30: Pinehurst No. 2 197
    Chapter 30 Answers: 201
    Did You Know? 202

CHAPTER 31: Royal County Down Golf Club 203
    Chapter 31 Answers: 208
    Did You Know? 209

CHAPTER 32: Muirfield 210
    Chapter 32 Answers: 215
    Did You Know? 216

CHAPTER 33: Carnoustie Golf Links 217
    Chapter 33 Answers: 221
    Did You Know? 222

CHAPTER 34: Unbeatable Records 223
    Chapter 34 Answers: 227
    Did You Know? 228

CONCLUSION 229

ATTENTION:
DO YOU WANT MY FUTURE BOOKS AT HEAVY DISCOUNTS AND EVEN FOR FREE?

HEAD OVER TO WWW.SECRETREADS.COM AND JOIN MY SECRET BOOK CLUB!

INTRODUCTION

For centuries, the game of golf was limited to individuals of wealth and status. Only in the past couple of decades has the game become more accessible to players without wealth and status, and with that newfound popularity, the game has continued to grow.

As the game is becoming more popular around the world, talented players are joining the ranks of the best. Some could argue that the golf being played today is the best it has ever been. Still, there is plenty of history behind the sport, and much of that history is worth remembering.

This book has 34 chapters of challenging questions, all focused on the great game of golf. The different chapters will span all of golf's history, so if you're not familiar with golf's past or its early days, then this is your chance to learn!

You'll be tested on the biggest names in golf history, including many of the major tournament champions over the years. There are also chapters dedicated to some of the most historic golf courses around the world.

Can you remember the biggest moments in golf, including incredible final-round moments that will be part of golf's history for decades to come? This book is going to test every aspect of your game, just like the biggest tournaments.

Consider this trivia quiz the biggest tournament of the year. It's the final round, and you're in position to win it all. Can you handle the pressure and bring it home? Time to tee it up and find out!

CHAPTER 1:
GOLF'S EARLY HISTORY

1. The Parliament of Scotland, led by which leader, was the first to ban golf on Sundays back in 1457?

   A. James I
   B. James II
   C. James III
   D. James IV

2. The golf ban in Scotland, which began in 1457, was not lifted until which year, by James IV, who initially upheld the ban?

   A. 1492
   B. 1499
   C. 1502
   D. 1507

3. Mary, Queen of Scots, was the first known female golfer when she was seen playing golf where in 1567?

   A. Seton Palace
   B. St. Andrews
   C. Scotscraig
   D. Montrose

4. The Royal Burgh of Edinburgh, in 1592, banned golf on which day of the week "in tyme of sermonis"?

   A. Thursdays
   B. Fridays
   C. Saturdays
   D. Sundays

5. King James VI of Scotland allowed the Scottish people to play golf on Sundays beginning in which year?

   A. 1618
   B. 1621
   C. 1633
   D. 1640

6. Charles I found out about which 1641 event while golfing, but decided he would finish his round before making any other decisions?

   A. Boston Tea Party
   B. Irish rebellion

C. Thirty Years' War
   D. Anglo-Spanish War

7. The first recorded international golf match took place in which year?

   A. 1682
   B. 1685
   C. 1690
   D. 1699

8. During that first international match, Andrew Dickson became the first documented what?

   A. Referee
   B. Greenskeeper
   C. Caddie
   D. Scorekeeper

9. The first written instructions on playing the sport of golf were written in which year?

   A. 1667
   B. 1687
   C. 1691
   D. 1696

10. Glasgow Green was the first named course on the west side of which country, back in 1721?

    A. England
    B. Ireland
    C. Spain
    D. Scotland

11. The first golf match ever reported upon in a newspaper took place during what year?

    A. 1724
    B. 1726
    C. 1730
    D. 1733

12. Which golf society formed in 1735 and claims to be the first golf society in the world?

    A. PGA of America

- B. Allied Golf Associations
- C. Royal Burgess Golf Society
- D. Honorable Company of Edinburgh Golfers

13. Thomas Mathison wrote an epic poem about golf back in 1743. About how many lines did his poem span?

    - A. 300
    - B. 400
    - C. 500
    - D. 600

14. The first golf club, as opposed to golf society, formed in 1744 at which golf course?

    - A. Muirfield
    - B. Carnoustie
    - C. Leith Links
    - D. St. Andrews

15. Bailie William Landale is the first champion at the first open championship competition at which course in 1754?

    - A. Musselburgh
    - B. Muirfield
    - C. Carnoustie
    - D. St. Andrews

16. Until 1759, what kind of play was the only kind of competition used in golf?

    - A. Stroke play
    - B. Match play
    - C. Skins
    - D. Best ball

17. In 1764, St. Andrews became the first course to have 18 holes. How many holes did the course have before going to 18?

    - A. 14
    - B. 16
    - C. 20
    - D. 22

18. The first golf clubhouse was erected in what year?

A. 1768
B. 1775
C. 1779
D. 1780

Chapter 1 Answers:

1. B. James II. He banned the game to keep his people's skills focused on archery, necessary for winning wars.
2. C. 1502. James IV is also remembered for purchasing the first set of golf clubs, made by a bow-maker in Perth, Scotland.
3. A. Seton Palace. It was not a golf club as they are recognized today, but she would go on retreats there and play on the property.
4. D. Sundays. The word "sermonis" means "sermons" in modern English, so they basically banned golf on Sundays to get more people to church.
5. A. 1618. The game was growing in popularity, so the pressure was on to keep people happy.
6. B. Irish rebellion. The moment marked the beginning of the English Civil War.
7. A. 1682. The Duke of York and John Paterson of Scotland were victorious over two English noblemen.
8. C. Caddie. He carried the bag for the Duke of York during the international match.
9. B. 1687. The instructions were found in a student diary written by Thomas Kincaid.
10. D. Scotland. In modern days, the area is a park, no longer used for golf.
11. A. 1724. Alexander Elphinstone and Captain John Porteous played what the newspaper called a "solemn match of golf."
12. C. Royal Burgess Golf Society. The Scottish golf club claims 1735, though their documentation only goes back to 1834.
13. A. 300. It is considered by most historians to be the first literary work dedicated to the game.
14. C. Leith Links. Today, though, the Honorable Company of Edinburgh Golfers calls Muirfield their home course.
15. D. St. Andrews. The golfers of the course purchased a Silver Cup to award to the annual winner of the competition.
16. B. Match play. The first written reference to stroke play was not made until 1759, and it grew in popularity from there.
17. D. 22. There were 11 holes out and 11 holes in, but then they combined the first four holes into two, reducing each side of the scorecard by two.
18. A. 1768. It was built at Leith Links, named the Golf House.

Did You Know?

In 1786, the South Carolina Golf Club became the first golf club to form outside of the United Kingdom.

CHAPTER 2:
Golf's Spread

1. The Kobe Golf Club, established in 1903, was the first to open in which country?

    A. China
    B. Japan
    C. South Korea
    D. Malaysia

2. Eight men founded which golf course in 1873, the first course in Canada?

    A. Royal Montreal Golf Club
    B. Royal Quebec Golf Club
    C. Toronto Golf Club
    D. Brantford Golf & Country Club

3. Which country's first golf course was the first to be founded outside of Great Britain?

    A. China
    B. Malaysia
    C. India
    D. United States

4. The Country Club was formed in 1882, making it the oldest in the history of the U.S. In which state can it be found?

    A. New York
    B. Illinois
    C. Pennsylvania
    D. Massachusetts

5. Spain's oldest golf course, The Real Club de Golf de Las Palmas, dates back to which year?

    A. 1891
    B. 1894
    C. 1899
    D. 1902

6. Pau Golf Club was founded in 1856, making it the first golf club in continental Europe. Which country was its home?

    A. Italy
    B. France

C. Belgium
D. Germany

7. The Royal Curragh Golf Club, founded in 1858, is located in which Irish county?

    A. Kilkenny
    B. Limerick
    C. Kildare
    D. Waterford

8. The Royal Adelaide Golf Club became the first golf club in Australia during what year?

    A. 1860
    B. 1863
    C. 1866
    D. 1870

9. How many years after Australia's first golf club did New Zealand establish its first golf club?

    A. One
    B. Two
    C. Three
    D. Four

10. The Royal Cape Golf Club was the first golf club in which country, and the first of its continent?

    A. South Africa
    B. Egypt
    C. Brazil
    D. Poland

11. John Hamilton Gillespie formed a golf course in Sarasota, Florida, in 1886. How many holes did it have?

    A. Two
    B. Four
    C. Six
    D. Nine

12. The Royal Malta Golf Club was formed in which year, making it Malta's first golf club?

A. 1884
   B. 1886
   C. 1887
   D. 1888

13. The Golfing Union of which country became the first golfing union in the world?

    A. Iceland
    B. Greenland
    C. Norway
    D. Ireland

14. Grand Duke Michael of Russia helped found which golf club in 1891?

    A. Royal Golf Club
    B. Cannes Golf Club
    C. Paris Golf Club
    D. Moscow Golf Club

15. Which country founded the first Ladies' Golf Union?

    A. England
    B. United States
    C. Scotland
    D. Ireland

16. The first golf club in Turkey was named what before changing its name along with its city?

    A. Bursa
    B. Istanbul
    C. Constantinople
    D. Ankara

17. Van Cortlandt Park Golf Course opened in 1895 in which American city?

    A. New York City
    B. Boston
    C. Chicago
    D. Atlanta

18. Golf was played for the first time at the Olympic Games in which city, back in 1900?

   A. St. Louis
   B. Paris
   C. Rome
   D. London

Chapter 2 Answers:

1. B. Japan. The golf course was designed by Arthur Hasketh Groom, from England. It started as a nine-hole course but expanded one year later.
2. A. Royal Montreal Golf Club. All four of the courses listed as choices were founded between 1873 and 1879.
3. C. India. The Royal Calcutta Golf Club was formed in 1829. Its 18 holes currently stretch for 7,195 yards.
4. D. Massachusetts. The Country Club is one of the five charter clubs that went on to found the United States Golf Association.
5. A. 1891. The course was located on the island of Gran Canaria.
6. B. France. Pau Golf Club was designed by Willie Dunn, and it is a private course adored for its beauty.
7. C. Kildare. The course is historically linked to the country's military, as it is located next to Curragh Camp.
8. D. 1870. The Royal Adelaide Golf Club was formed by a group of more than 20 politicians, and Sir James Fergusson, the Governor, served as the club's patron.
9. A. One. The Otago Golf Club was formed in 1871, just one year after Australia's first golf club.
10. A. South Africa. The first club in Africa was formed in 1885 in Wynberg, South Africa.
11. A. Two. The course was located on Gillespie's personal property, and he would go on to build more.
12. D. 1888. It was formed by a British soldier, as many of these golf clubs around the world tended to be.
13. D. Ireland. It was formed in October 1891, before any other country could form a golf union.
14. B. Cannes Golf Club. It was formed in 1891, and the Grand Duke also taught Prince Albert how to play the game.
15. D. Ireland. It was formed in 1893, only two years after the first golf union.
16. C. Constantinople. It was formed in 1895 but is known as the IGK today, for the Istanbul Golf Club.
17. A. New York City. It became the first public golf course in the United States.
18. B. Paris. There was a 36-hole stroke play competition for the men and a nine-hole stroke play competition for the women.

Did You Know?

All three medals at the 1900 Olympic Games for women's golf were won by Americans, including Margaret Abbott, who won the gold medal.

CHAPTER 3:
The Early Open Championship Years

1. The first Open Championship was held in which year, and nearly every year since then?
   - A. 1860
   - B. 1861
   - C. 1862
   - D. 1863

2. In the very first Open Championship, which player was victorious by two strokes?
   - A. Old Tom Morris
   - B. Willie Park Sr.
   - C. Andrew Strath
   - D. Young Tom Morris

3. How many players entered the first Open Championship?
   - A. Five
   - B. Seven
   - C. Eight
   - D. Ten

4. Though Old Tom Morris was unsuccessful at his first Open Championship, how many of the first eight did he win?
   - A. Two
   - B. Three
   - C. Four
   - D. Five

5. How many Open Championships were played without a prize purse?
   - A. One
   - B. Two
   - C. Three
   - D. Four

6. In 1871, there was no Open Championship for what reason?
   - A. War in Europe
   - B. No trophy available
   - C. No participants
   - D. Pandemic

7. Out of the first ten Open Championship winners, which player only won one of them?

    A. Willie Park Sr.
    B. Old Tom Morris
    C. Andrew Strath
    D. Young Tom Morris

8. Which player finished as the runner-up twice in a row, in 1869 and 1870, but never won an Open Championship?

    A. Davie Strath
    B. Jamie Anderson
    C. Bob Kirk
    D. Davie Park

9. Which of these courses was the first, besides Prestwick, to host the Open Championship?

    A. Musselburgh
    B. St. Andrews
    C. Muirfield
    D. St. George's

10. How many Open Championships did Young Tom Morris win in a row, beginning in 1868?

    A. Three
    B. Four
    C. Five
    D. Six

11. Which Open Championship was the first to require a playoff to decide a winner?

    A. 14th
    B. 15th
    C. 16th
    D. 17th

12. Who was the first non-Scottish player to win the Open Championship?

    A. John Ball
    B. Harold Hilton

C. John Henry Taylor
D. Harry Vardon

13. Which of these Open Championships was the first hosted by Musselburgh Links?

    A. 11th
    B. 12th
    C. 13th
    D. 14th

14. For the 40th Open Championship, in 1900, how much was the prize purse, in pounds?

    A. £100
    B. £125
    C. £150
    D. £200

15. From 1894 to 1900, the Open Championship was won by Englishmen seven years in a row. Which of these men is not one of them?

    A. John Henry Taylor
    B. Harry Vardon
    C. Jack Burns
    D. Harold Hilton

16. In what year did the tournament switch from a 36-hole tournament to 72 holes, played in two days?

    A. 1890
    B. 1892
    C. 1895
    D. 1900

17. In 1907, a player from which country was the first non-Scottish and non-English player to win the Open Championship?

    A. France
    B. United States
    C. Argentina
    D. South Africa

18. Harry Vardon won more Open Championships than any other player. How many did he win?

   A. Four
   B. Five
   C. Six
   D. Seven

Chapter 3 Answers:

1. A. 1860. The competition was held at Prestwick Golf Club, in Scotland.
2. B. Willie Park Sr. He had a total of 174 strokes, and Old Tom Morris finished in second place.
3. C. Eight. The players competed over three rounds of 12 holes each.
4. C. Four. He even won the third Open Championship, in 1862, by a total of 13 strokes.
5. C. Three. The first Open Championship to award a prize purse was the fourth, in 1863. Willie Park Sr. won £10.
6. B. No trophy available. Instead of just competing for money, the tournament was canceled altogether. The tournament would not be canceled again until World War I.
7. C. Andrew Strath. He won the Sixth Open Championship over Willie Park Sr., though he would not win it again.
8. C. Bob Kirk. He was second to Young Tom Morris by 11 and 12 strokes. Davie Strath also finished as runner-up twice in a row, in 1870 and 1871.
9. B. St. Andrews. It was the 13th Open Championship in 1873, won by Tom Kidd.
10. B. Four. In his first Open Championship, he finished three strokes ahead of his father, Old Tom Morris, for the victory.
11. C. 16th. Bob Martin defeated Davie Strath in 1876, claiming his prize of £8.
12. A. John Ball. He won the 30th Open Championship, in 1889, as an amateur. He would finish as the runner-up two years later, then never win again.
13. D. 14th. Mungo Park won the championship over Young Tom Morris by a total of two strokes.
14. B. £125. The winner took home £50, while the rest was dispersed among the runners-up.
15. C. Jack Burns. Burns won the 28th Open as a Scotsman, while the other three men split those seven Open Championships from 1894 to 1900.
16. B. 1892. Up to that time, Young Tom Morris was the only player to win a tournament with a total score of less than 150. He shot 149 in 1870, when he won by 12 strokes.

17. A. France. Amaud Massy finished two strokes ahead of John Henry Taylor to win the 46th Open Championship at Royal Liverpool.
18. C. Six. His sixth win came in 1914 during the 54th Open Championship, the last tournament before World War I broke out. James Braid is second on the list with five championships.

Did You Know?

Young Tom Morris was the youngest winner, at 17 years and 156 days, while Old Tom Morris was the oldest winner, at 46 years and 102 days.

CHAPTER 4:
The Amateur Championship

1. The Royal Liverpool Golf Club organized the first Amateur Championship back in which year?

    A. 1880
    B. 1882
    C. 1884
    D. 1885

2. Unlike the Open Championship, the Amateur Championship used what form of competition?

    A. Skins
    B. Match
    C. Stroke
    D. Scramble

3. In the first Amateur Championship, when two players were tied at the end of their round, how was the winner determined?

    A. Coin toss
    B. Rematch in the next round
    C. Playoff holes
    D. Fewest putts

4. Which player won the first Amateur Championship by a score of seven and six?

    A. Horace Hutchinson
    B. John Ball
    C. Allan Macfie
    D. Henry Lamb

5. Through 2024, how many different courses have hosted the Amateur Championship?

    A. 21
    B. 22
    C. 23
    D. 24

6. Which of these courses has hosted the Amateur Championship more than any other course?

    A. St. Andrews
    B. Royal Liverpool

C. Royal St. George's
   D. Prestwick

7. How many players have won the Amateur Championship more than once?

   A. 16
   B. 17
   C. 18
   D. 19

8. Which player has won more Amateur Championships than any other?

   A. John Ball
   B. Michael Bonallack
   C. Harold Hilton
   D. Joe Carr

9. Only once in Amateur Championship history has the final required three playoff holes. Who won that playoff?

   A. Michael Lunt
   B. Martin Christmas
   C. John Hall
   D. Gordon Clark

10. Sometimes, a championship match isn't very competitive. What is the biggest margin of victory in an Amateur Championship final?

    A. 11 and ten
    B. 13 and 12
    C. 14 and 13
    D. 15 and 14

11. The last player to win his second Amateur Championship was Gary Wolstenholme. In what year did he win it?

    A. 1991
    B. 2003
    C. 2005
    D. 2007

12. The first American to reach the Amateur Championship final match was Walter Travis. In what year did he accomplish this?

A. 1904
B. 1912
C. 1916
D. 1930

13. Though Travis was the first American to reach and win the Amateur final, which American was next to reach the final?

    A. Douglas Grant
    B. Jess Sweetser
    C. Robert A. Gardner
    D. Bobby Jones

14. With winners from Scotland, England, and the United States dominating the Amateur Championship, a player from which country won the first Amateur Championship after World War II?

    A. New Zealand
    B. Wales
    C. Australia
    D. Ireland

15. Peter McEvoy was the last player to win the Amateur Championship two years in a row. Which year marked his second win?

    A. 1973
    B. 1978
    C. 1984
    D. 1989

16. How many players in golf history have won both the Amateur Championship and the Open Championship?

    A. Two
    B. Three
    C. Four
    D. Five

17. From 1983 to 2019, the Amateur Championship held how many rounds of qualifying stroke play for each tournament?

    A. One
    B. Two
    C. Three

D. Four

18. The first player to lead the stroke-play qualifying also went on to win the Amateur Championship. Who was it?
    A. Dana Banke
    B. Philip Parkin
    C. Andrew Hare
    D. Stephen Dodd

Chapter 4 Answers:

1. D. 1885. The first tournament was held on April 20, 21, and 23 of that year, and it was open to any amateur player who was a member of a recognized golf club.
2. B. Match. Players were paired randomly in each round, and any odd player left out earned a bye to the next round.
3. B. Rematch in the next round. Both players would advance but have to play against each other again.
4. C. Allan Macfie. The Scottish player would not win the championship ever again, but the first one, held at Royal Liverpool, was his.
5. C. 23. Royal Aberdeen Golf Club, Royal Dornoch Golf Club, and Ballyliffin Golf Club have each hosted the tournament only once.
6. B. Royal Liverpool. As of 2024, it has hosted the tournament 18 times, while St. Andrews has played host 16 times.
7. A. 16. Of those 16 players, only four of them have won the Amateur Championship more than twice.
8. A. John Ball. He won the Amateur Championship eight times. Bonallack has five wins, Hilton has four, and Carr has three.
9. D. Gordon Clark. He defeated Michael Lunt on the 39th hole of their competition, winning the 1964 Amateur Championship.
10. C. 14 and 13. Lawson Little made quick work of his match with James Wallace to win the 1934 Amateur Championship.
11. B. 2003. Wolstenholme won his second Amateur Championship 12 years after his first in 1991.
12. A. 1904. Travis defeated Edward Blackwell 4 & 3 at Royal St George's.
13. C. Robert A. Gardner. He reached the final in 1920, losing to Cyril Tolley in 37 holes at Muirfield.
14. D. Ireland. Jimmy Bruen defeated Robert Sweeny Jr. four and three at Royal Birkdale. Another Irish player would win in 1953, seven years later.
15. B. 1978. He defeated Hugh Campbell in 1977 and Paul McKellar in 1978.
16. B. Three. John Ball, Harold Hilton, and Bobby Jones have all been successful in winning both tournaments. Of those three players, Bobby Jones had the fewest Amateur wins, with one.

17. B. Two. They had to reduce the number of qualifiers with the stroke play, and they reduced the stroke play rounds to one in 2020.
18. B. Philip Parkin. He also led the qualifier in 1984, but he did not win the championship that year.

Did You Know?

Matteo Manassero also led the qualifying portion before going on to win the Amateur back in 2009, defeating Sam Hutsby in the final at Formby.

CHAPTER 5: THE 1890S

1. In 1890, the idea of what came around, but they called it a "Ground Score"?

   A. Par
   B. Birdie
   C. Handicap
   D. Eagle

2. In 1891, which famous golf club was founded on Long Island in New York?

   A. Augusta National
   B. Torrey Pines
   C. Shinnecock Hills
   D. TPC Sawgrass

3. Which golf club, known for hosting the oldest known golf tournament in the United States, was founded in 1892?

   A. Shinnecock Hills
   B. Augusta National
   C. Torrey Pines
   D. Oakhurst

4. The first international championship event was founded in 1892 in which country?

   A. England
   B. India
   C. Scotland
   D. United States

5. The Chicago Golf Club opened the United States' first 18-hole course in 1893, but it moved to its current location in which year?

   A. 1894
   B. 1895
   C. 1899
   D. 1906

6. Which golf course hosted the first British Ladies Amateur Golf Championship in 1893?

   A. Royal Lytham & St Annes
   B. Cannes

C. Coventry
D. Berkhamsted

7. In 1894, the Open Championship was played on a course in which country for the first time?

   A. Ireland
   B. England
   C. Scotland
   D. France

8. Which of these golf courses was not a founding member of the Amateur Golf Association of the United States?

   A. Newport Country Club
   B. St. Andrew's Golf Club
   C. Shinnecock Hills Golf Club
   D. Victoria Golf Club

9. In Springfield Center, New York, the Otsego Golf Club opened in 1894 with how many holes?

   A. Nine
   B. 12
   C. 14
   D. 18

10. Tacoma Golf Club was founded in 1894, the first golf club in which region?

    A. U.S. Pacific Coast
    B. Canadian Atlantic Coast
    C. Eastern France
    D. Southern Italy

11. In 1895, the USGA ruled that what could not be used as a putter on the golf course?

    A. Hockey stick
    B. Tennis racket
    C. Pool cue
    D. Baseball bat

12. In 1895, the U.S. Amateur was founded and held for the first time, one day before which tournament was also held for the first time?

A. The Masters
B. The Players
C. U.S. Open
D. PGA Championship

13. Louis Bayard Jr. won the first NCAA Golf Championship in which year?

    A. 1896
    B. 1897
    C. 1898
    D. 1899

14. Atlantic C. C. was the site where which golf term was coined in 1898?

    A. Bogey
    B. Birdie
    C. Eagle
    D. Par

15. Freddie Tait had a bet that he could reach the Royal Cinque Ports Golf Club from the Royal St George's Golf Club, three miles away, in less than 40 golf shots. How many did he need to do it?

    A. 32
    B. 38
    C. 41
    D. 44

16. The Haskell ball was invented in 1898, and it was the first to have what kind of core?

    A. Cork
    B. Dried sap
    C. Wood
    D. Rubber

17. The Western Open was played for the first time in 1899 in which state?

    A. Illinois
    B. Indiana
    C. Michigan
    D. Nebraska

18. The U.S. Women's Amateur was founded in 1895. Who won the inaugural competition?
    A. Frances C. Griscom
    B. Ruth Underhill
    C. Beatrix Hoyt
    D. Lucy Barnes Brown

Chapter 5 Answers:

1. C. Handicap. It was developed by Hugh Rotherham, who was a member of the Coventry Golf Club.
2. C. Shinnecock Hills. The course would go on to host the second U.S. Open in 1896.
3. D. Oakhurst. The Oakhurst Challenge Medal is the oldest known prize for golf in the United States.
4. B. India. The Amateur Golf Championship of India and the East was the first to invite players from multiple countries.
5. B. 1895. The Chicago Golf Club was originally built where Downers Grove Golf Course now resides.
6. A. Royal Lytham & St Annes. The first tournament was won by Lady Margaret Scott.
7. B. England. J. H. Taylor won the tournament, and Taylor, Harry Vardon, and James Braid would be the dominant players on the scene for almost 20 years.
8. D. Victoria Golf Club. The Amateur Golf Association would eventually be renamed to the United States Golf Association.
9. B. 12. The course has operated non-stop since 1894, and it operates as a nine-hole course today.
10. A. U.S. Pacific Coast. Today, the Tacoma Country & Golf Club is a private club with an 18-hole course with nearly 7,000 yards of play.
11. C. Pool cue. Golfers must have liked the idea of lining up their putts just as it's done in the pool hall!
12. C. U.S. Open. Horace Rawlins won the first U.S. Open, while Charles B. Macdonald won the first U.S. Amateur.
13. B. 1897. It was held at the Ardsley Club in New York, and Yale won the team championship.
14. B. Birdie. Players at the course would compliment a great hole by saying it was "a bird of a hole."
15. A. 32. His 32nd shot went through a window at the Cinque Ports Golf Clubhouse, so he won the bet.
16. D. Rubber. The invention has lasted as the standard for the modern golf ball, though it has been adjusted over time.
17. A. Illinois. It was the first tournament that would become part of what is known as the PGA Tour.
18. D. Lucy Barnes Brown. She won the contest with 132 strokes over 18 holes, as match play was not used until the next year.

Did You Know?

Bogey was initially a term for how many strokes a good golfer should take to complete a hole, similar to par and birdie as they are understood today.

CHAPTER 6: THE 1900S

1. In the year 1900, Harry Vardon won which event, marking an early historic moment in golf?

    A. The Open
    B. Amateur Championship
    C. U.S. Amateur
    D. U.S. Open

2. The first Professional Golfers' Association was formed in which year?

    A. 1900
    B. 1901
    C. 1902
    D. 1903

3. Though the rubber core golf ball was invented a few years earlier, the first player to win a major title with it won which tournament?

    A. U.S. Open
    B. U.S. Amateur
    C. Amateur Championship
    D. British Open

4. Sunningdale opened for play in 1901, the first golf course that used only what?

    A. Grass seed
    B. Meadows
    C. Par-three holes
    D. Chipping clubs

5. In 1901, Donald Ross completed his first golf course design in Pinehurst, North Carolina. How many courses would he complete as an architect over his career?

    A. 300
    B. 400
    C. 500
    D. 600

6. In 1902, the first Amateur Team competition was held in Europe, with which team winning?

    A. England
    B. Ireland
    C. Scotland

D. United States

7. In 1903, irons with what feature made their debut?

    A. Club grips
    B. Different face angles
    C. Shaft lengths
    D. Grooved faces

8. In 1903, Oakmont Country Club was founded in which U.S. state?

    A. New York
    B. Pennsylvania
    C. Massachusetts
    D. Maine

9. Which player was the first to win the British Amateur while using a center-shafted putter in 1904?

    A. Walter Travis
    B. Robert Maxwell
    C. Sandy Herd
    D. Laurie Auchterlonie

10. Women golfers from Britain and the U.S. played a match in which year?

    A. 1904
    B. 1905
    C. 1906
    D. 1907

11. Who patented the first dimple pattern on the ball in 1905, marking another change in golf balls?

    A. Harry Vardon
    B. Arnaud Massy
    C. Robert Maxwell
    D. William Taylor

12. Jack Oke of England won which tournament in 1904, the first time it was ever held?

    A. Mexico Open
    B. Canadian Open
    C. Scottish Open
    D. Puerto Rico Open

13. Goodrich invented a golf ball that had a rubber core filled with compressed air, but they sometimes did what in warm weather?

    A. Deflate
    B. Explode
    C. Malfunction
    D. Float

14. Which golf tournament was canceled when a dispute over its format could not be resolved?

    A. 1908 Summer Olympics
    B. 1907 U.S. Open
    C. 1907 British Open
    D. 1909 Canadian Open

15. Which woman became the first female professional in 1908?

    A. Mrs. William Taylor
    B. Mrs. Gordon Robertson
    C. Mrs. Walter Travis
    D. Mrs. Robert Maxwell

16. Walter Travis launched what magazine in 1908, one of his many golf publications?

    A. *The Mystery of Golf*
    B. *Golf*
    C. *The American Golfer*
    D. *The Complete Golfer*

17. Harry Vardon published what in 1905, which helped promote his interlocking golf grip?

    A. *The Mystery of Golf*
    B. *Golf*
    C. *Practical Golf*
    D. *The Complete Golfer*

18. Which of these groups were not considered golf professionals by a new rule from the USGA in 1909?

    A. Caddies
    B. Caddymasters
    C. Greenkeepers
    D. Rangers

Chapter 6 Answers:

1. D. U.S. Open. While it might not seem important on its own, Vardon was the first player in golf history to have won both the Open and the U.S. Open.
2. B. 1901. Though the first PGA was for Great Britain and Ireland, it does not have to specify that in its title since it was the first one to form.
3. B. U.S. Amateur. Walter Travis won the 1901 U.S. Amateur, but when both the British Open and U.S. Open winners in 1902 also used the ball, almost all players adopted it.
4. A. Grass seed. Before this course opened, golf courses were often routed through natural meadows, which caused drainage problems from the clay underneath.
5. D. 600. He was named to the World Golf Hall of Fame in 1977 for his efforts.
6. C. Scotland. The current international championships wouldn't take place until the 1950s.
7. D. Grooved faces. It was another step toward the modern game and players gaining more control over their golf shots.
8. B. Pennsylvania. It was designed by Henry Fownes and is praised for its beauty to this day.
9. A. Walter Travis. He was also the first player to win three U.S. Amateur titles, which he had accomplished the year previous.
10. B. 1905. The British women won by a commanding score of six matches to one.
11. D. William Taylor. It was quickly adopted by many players for its improved flight through the air.
12. B. Canadian Open. Oke won the event with a score of +16, edging out Percy Barrett by two strokes at the Royal Montreal.
13. B. Explode. Even with the ball in a player's pocket, it could explode, so as you can imagine, the ball was eventually discontinued.
14. A. 1908 Summer Olympics. It was a poor moment in golf history, limiting its appeal around the world.
15. B. Mrs. Gordon Robertson. She played out of Princes Ladies Golf Club, which would host a Match Play Championship a few years later.
16. C. *The American Golfer*. The other choices were all publications of one kind or another in the 1900s.

17. D. *The Complete Golfer*. Vardon's grip remains one of the most popular in modern golf, even after more than 100 years.
18. D. Rangers. Any of the other three choices who were over 16 were considered professionals until the rule was removed in 1963.

Did You Know?

While golf did not work out at the 1908 Summer Olympics, it had made its second appearance at the 1904 Summer Olympics in St. Louis.

CHAPTER 7: THE 1910S

1. In 1910, the R&A banned what, marking the first time that the R&A and the USGA had differing golf rules?

    A. Groove-faced irons
    B. Metal drivers
    C. Center-shafted putter
    D. Compressed air balls

2. John McDermott was the first native-born American to win which tournament in 1911?

    A. U.S. Open
    B. British Open
    C. U.S. Amateur
    D. Canadian Open

3. Arthur F. Knight patented what improvement to the golf club in 1910?

    A. Carbon fiber shaft
    B. Steel shaft
    C. Shaft flex
    D. Adjustable club face

4. The United States established its first national handicapping system in what year?

    A. 1911
    B. 1912
    C. 1913
    D. 1914

5. The first professional match between two international teams took place in 1913 between France and which country?

    A. India
    B. Ireland
    C. England
    D. United States

6. In 1913, which player became the first amateur to win the U.S. Open?

    A. Harry Vardon
    B. John Ball
    C. Francis Ouimet
    D. John McDermott

7. Which golf club was formed at Komazawa in 1914?

    A. Komazawa Golf Club
    B. Tokyo Golf Club
    C. Kanto Golf Club
    D. Hodogaya Country Club

8. In 1915, the Open Championship was paused for what event?

    A. World War I
    B. World War II
    C. Spanish Flu
    D. Titanic crash

9. Harry Vardon won the Open Championship again in 1914. How many more than Tom Watson did he win?

    A. One
    B. Two
    C. Three
    D. Four

10. How many charter members were involved in the founding of the PGA of America?

    A. 65
    B. 74
    C. 82
    D. 95

11. In 1916, the first PGA Championship was won by which player?

    A. Jock Hutchison
    B. Fred McLeod
    C. Jim Barnes
    D. Walter Hagen

12. Francis Ouimet was briefly banned from amateur play for what reason in 1916?

    A. Involvement with the sporting goods business
    B. Sports gambling
    C. Accepting payments
    D. Sponsorships

13. The first American miniature golf course opened in 1916 in which U.S. state?

A. North Carolina
B. South Carolina
C. Georgia
D. Mississippi

14. The Open Championship was paused for World War I in 1915, but in what year did the PGA Championship and U.S. Open do the same?

    A. 1915
    B. 1916
    C. 1917
    D. 1918

15. Walter Hagen won his first U.S. Open in which year, defeating Chick Evans by one stroke?

    A. 1914
    B. 1915
    C. 1916
    D. 1919

16. Who did Walter Hagen defeat in a playoff to capture the 1919 U.S. Open?

    A. Jock Hutchison
    B. Mike Brady
    C. Jerome Travers
    D. Chick Evans

17. Which of these players won their first British Open in 1912?

    A. James Braid
    B. Harry Vardon
    C. John Henry Taylor
    D. Ted Ray

18. Ted Ray tried to repeat as British Open Champion in 1913, but he lost to which player by eight strokes?

    A. Harry Vardon
    B. John Henry Taylor
    C. James Braid
    D. Sandy Herd

Chapter 7 Answers:

1. C. Center-shafted putter. The ban lasted for nearly 20 years but was eventually revoked.
2. A. U.S. Open. Also, he was only 19 when he won the tournament, making him the youngest to ever do so.
3. B. Steel shaft. It was a significant step toward the modern game, showing how technology and manufacturing were helping the game make strides forward.
4. A. 1911. Though the handicap system struggled to gain traction, adjustments allowed weaker players to feel the benefits.
5. D. United States. The match took place at La Boulie Golf Club in France.
6. C. Francis Ouimet. He defeated Harry Vardon and Ted Ray in a playoff to capture the victory.
7. B. Tokyo Golf Club. The club would be moved over the years, but that first club is seen as the launching point for the golfing craze in Japan.
8. A. World War I. Many events were paused around the world for the Great War, and golf was no exception.
9. A. One. Harry Vardon won six Open Championships, while Tom Watson won five in a much more competitive era.
10. C. 82. The strong charter allowed for the founding and inauguration of the PGA Championship.
11. C. Jim Barnes. He defeated Jock Hutchison one up in the final match, which took place at the Siwanoy Country Club.
12. A. Involvement with the sporting goods business. His ban caused protests, so it was reversed two years later.
13. A. North Carolina. It opened in the city of Pinehurst and was called Thistle Dhu.
14. C. 1917. The two tournaments would remain canceled until 1919.
15. A. 1914. Hagen shot 290 during the tournament that took place at Midlothian, in Illinois.
16. B. Mike Brady. Hagen finished with a 301 score; 11 strokes worse than his win five years before.
17. D. Ted Ray. He shot 295, four shots better than Harry Vardon, who was trying to win his sixth Open Championship.

18. B. John Henry Taylor. It was Taylor's fifth Open Championship win, and it would be his last. Ray would not win again either, though he would fall only one stroke short in 1925.

Did You Know?

The Open Championship did not hold a tournament in 1919 due to World War I, though the U.S. Open and PGA Championship were able to restart play that year.

CHAPTER 8:
THE 1920S

1. The USGA created what section, named for a color, to conduct research on turfgrass?

    A. Yellow
    B. Brown
    C. Blue
    D. Green

2. A golf tournament was scheduled for the 1920 Summer Olympics in which city?

    A. Antwerp
    B. London
    C. Madrid
    D. Oslo

3. Walter Hagen became the first native-born American to do what in 1922?

    A. Win the PGA Championship
    B. Win the Open Championship
    C. Win the Canadian Open
    D. Be expelled from professional golf

4. In 1922, which match, between two teams of amateur golfers, took place for the first time?

    A. Ryder Cup
    B. Curtis Cup
    C. Walker Cup
    D. Solheim Cup

5. The Texas Open, the second-oldest surviving PGA Tour event, debuted in which year?

    A. 1922
    B. 1923
    C. 1924
    D. 1927

6. The West and East courses at which golf club opened for play in 1923?

    A. Augusta National
    B. Pinehurst

C. Torrey Pines
   D. Winged Foot

7. In 1924, Joyce Wethered set a record by winning the English Ladies' Championship how many consecutive times?

   A. Three
   B. Four
   C. Five
   D. Six

8. The USGA legalized steel shafted golf clubs in 1925, how many years ahead of the R&A across the ocean?

   A. Three
   B. Four
   C. Five
   D. Six

9. In 1925, the first fairway irrigation system was developed in which U.S. city?

   A. Orlando
   B. Dallas
   C. Boston
   D. New York

10. Though they disagreed on steel shafts, both the USGA and R&A banned deep-grooved irons in what year?

    A. 1925
    B. 1928
    C. 1929
    D. 1935

11. In 1926, which event took place for the first time, the first event to offer a purse of $10,000?

    A. Bing Crosby Pro-Am
    B. Hershey Open
    C. Texas Open
    D. Los Angeles Open

12. Walter Hagen and Bobby Jones played a privately sponsored match. How many holes was the match?

A. 18
B. 36
C. 54
D. 72

13. The first Ryder Cup matches were played in 1927. How many points did the USA score in their victory?

    A. 7
    B. 8.5
    C. 9.5
    D. 10

14. Creeping bentgrass was developed by the U.S. Department of Agriculture for use on which part of the golf course?

    A. Rough
    B. Greens
    C. Fairways
    D. Tees

15. After their 1927 loss, Great Britain would return the favor in the Ryder Cup's next iteration, in 1929. How many points of the possible 12 did they score in their victory?

    A. 7
    B. 8
    C. 9
    D. 10.5

16. Walter Hagen won the Open Championship in 1929. By that time, how many times had he won it?

    A. Three
    B. Four
    C. Five
    D. Six

17. Who won the Open Championship on both ends of Hagen's victories in 1928 and 1929?

    A. Bobby Jones
    B. Jim Barnes
    C. Tommy Armour
    D. Gene Sarazen

18. Great Britain and Ireland got their first standardized handicap system in which year?

    A. 1922
    B. 1924
    C. 1926
    D. 1928

Chapter 8 Answers:

1. D. Green. The Green Section has become a famous part of the organization, helping golf courses grow with success all over the country.
2. A. Antwerp. Though the tournament was scheduled, it was once again canceled, taking golf out of the Olympics.
3. B. Win the Open Championship. He used his standing in the world of golf to start a golf equipment company under his name.
4. C. Walker Cup. The United States and Great Britain/Ireland compete for the cup every two years.
5. A. 1922. The tournament's first winner was Bob MacDonald, who scored one stroke better than Cyril Walker.
6. D. Winged Foot. They were designed by A. W. Tillinghast.
7. C. Five. Interestingly, she defeated a different opponent in the final for each of those championship victories.
8. C. Five. The Rules of Golf diverged in those five years, adding difficulties to players who were competing on both sides of the ocean.
9. B. Dallas. With the ability to water areas that needed it, golf courses gained the freedom to survive almost anywhere.
10. A. 1925. The two associations took another step toward a standard set of rules to govern the game.
11. D. Los Angeles Open. Today, the tournament is known as the Genesis Invitational, and it has also been called the Genesis Open, Northern Trust Open, and Nissan Open.
12. D. 72. Hagen defeated Jones 12 and 11 in the match.
13. C. 9.5. They soundly defeated the British team, led by their captain, Walter Hagen.
14. B. Greens. The U.S. government was helping the growth and quality of the sport, aiding its popularity in modern times.
15. A. 7. It was a closer match, but the British team was able to prevail on their home turf, in Yorkshire.
16. B. Four. It was the last time he would win the tournament.
17. A. Bobby Jones. Jones won the tournament three times, all as an amateur.
18. C. 1926. It took them 15 years longer than the United States, but it was still a positive step to help golf grow for all skill levels.

Did You Know?

George Herbert Walker Bush, 41st President of the United States, is a direct descendant of the founder of the Walker Cup, George Herbert Walker.

CHAPTER 9:
THE 1930S

1. Bobby Jones completed the original Grand Slam in 1930. Which of these tournaments was not part of that accomplishment?

    A. PGA Championship
    B. U.S. Open
    C. British Open
    D. British Amateur

2. After completing the Grand Slam, Bobby Jones retired from golf but also helped to found a new golf club that eventually became which iconic course?

    A. Torrey Pines
    B. Augusta National
    C. Pebble Beach
    D. Bethpage Black

3. Which of these golf tournaments did Gene Sarazen win in 1933?

    A. Masters
    B. PGA Championship
    C. U.S. Open
    D. The Open Championship

4. Gene Sarazen also won the 1932 U.S. Open. How many shots ahead of second place did he finish?

    A. One
    B. Two
    C. Three
    D. Four

5. Denny Shute had 17 professional wins as a golfer. How many of those wins were majors, all of which occurred in the 1930s?

    A. Two
    B. Three
    C. Four
    D. Five

6. What year did Augusta National open?

    A. 1931
    B. 1932
    C. 1933
    D. 1939

7. Who hit the "Shot Heard 'Round the World" at the 1935 Masters Tournament?

   A. Tommy Armour
   B. Horton Smith
   C. Henry Cotton
   D. Gene Sarazen

8. Who defeated Patty Berg to win her sixth U.S. Women's Amateur title in 1935?

   A. Glenna Collett-Vare
   B. Virginia Van Wie
   C. Helen Hicks
   D. Pam Barton

9. Who won the U.S. Amateur two years in a row, in 1934 and 1935?

   A. David Goldman
   B. Lawson Little
   C. Johnny Fischer
   D. Bud Ward

10. How many times did Walter Hagen win the PGA Championship during the 1930s?

    A. Zero
    B. One
    C. Two
    D. Three

11. When was the last time a player won a major championship using hickory-shafted clubs?

    A. 1933
    B. 1936
    C. 1938
    D. 1939

12. In 1934, the PGA Tour was created. In the same year, which player won the first-ever Masters tournament?

    A. Paul Runyan
    B. Henry Cotton
    C. Horton Smith
    D. Olin Dutra

13. Which golfer led the PGA Tour's Money List in the Tour's first year of operation?

    A. Craig Wood
    B. Harry Cooper
    C. Henry Cotton
    D. Paul Runyan

14. Which company became the first official sponsor of a professional golf tournament in 1933?

    A. *LIFE Magazine*
    B. KitchenAid
    C. Hershey Chocolate Company
    D. Valero Oil Company

15. In what year did Sam Snead first lead the PGA Tour Money List?

    A. 1935
    B. 1936
    C. 1938
    D. 1939

16. Which Pro-Am was created in San Diego, back in 1937?

    A. Bing Crosby
    B. Bobby Jones
    C. Clark Gable
    D. Cary Grant

17. Who won the 1938 Open Championship, with a winning score of +15?

    A. Jimmy Adams
    B. Reg Whitcombe
    C. Henry Cotton
    D. Alf Perry

18. Who won the 1939 U.S. Open at the Philadelphia Country Club?

    A. Ralph Guldahl
    B. Craig Wood
    C. Denny Shute
    D. Byron Nelson

Chapter 9 Answers:

1. A. PGA Championship. The other three choices, along with the U.S. Amateur, comprised the first Grand Slam of golf.
2. B. Augusta National. Jones retired from golf at 28 years old, leaving him plenty of time to work as a lawyer and enjoy the game of golf.
3. B. PGA Championship. Sarazen then won the Masters in 1935, finishing his career with seven major victories. He was selected to the World Golf Hall of Fame in 1974.
4. C. Three. Bobby Cruickshank and Philip Perkins finished tied at +9, while Sarazen won with a score of +6.
5. B. Three. Shute won the 1936 and 1937 PGA Championships, along with the 1933 Open Championship.
6. C. 1933. The course was designed by Alister MacKenzie, though Bobby Jones provided advice along the way.
7. D. Gene Sarazen. The famous shot was a double eagle on the par-five 15th hole, which helped propel him to victory.
8. A. Glenna Collett-Vare. She won the match three and two at the Interlachen Country Club in Minnesota.
9. B. Lawson Little. He defeated David Goldman eight and seven in 1934, then he defeated Walter Emery four and two in 1936.
10. A. Zero. The last time Walter Hagen won the PGA Championship was 1927, when he won it for the fourth time in a row.
11. B. 1936. Johnny Fischer won the U.S. Amateur with hickory-shafted clubs, the last hurrah before steel shafts dominated the scene entirely.
12. C. Horton Smith. He finished with a score of -4, two strokes ahead of Craig Wood.
13. D. Paul Runyan. He finished the season with $6,767 in winnings.
14. C. Hershey Chocolate Company. The Hershey Open was held from 1933 to 1941, and the first winner was Ed Dudley.
15. C. 1938. He turned pro in 1934, then led the PGA in earnings during the 1938 season. His first major championship would come a few years later.
16. A. Bing Crosby. Though the tournament moved from San Diego to the Monterey Peninsula a few years later, the tournament is still played every year.
17. B. Reg Whitcombe. He won by two strokes in what was a difficult set of course conditions.

18. D. Byron Nelson. He won in a playoff against both Craig Wood and Denny Shute.

Did You Know?

The USGA instituted the 14-club rule in 1938, and they also began allowing players to mark and move balls within six inches of the hole, regardless of distance to the next-closest ball. Before that, players had to chip over or putt around other balls on the green!

CHAPTER 10:
THE 1940S

1. For how many years was the Open Championship not played because of World War II?

   A. Three
   B. Four
   C. Five
   D. Six

2. How many times did Jimmy Demaret win the Masters during the 1940s?

   A. One
   B. Two
   C. Three
   D. Four

3. In 1944, the PGA Tour expanded its number of events to how many, even though many of their star players were fighting in the war?

   A. 18
   B. 20
   C. 22
   D. 24

4. Byron Nelson set the PGA Tour record for most consecutive wins in 1945. How many wins did he string together?

   A. Seven
   B. Ten
   C. 11
   D. 14

5. Byron Nelson led the PGA Tour Money List twice in the 1940s, but which year earned him the most money?

   A. 1944
   B. 1945
   C. 1947
   D. 1949

6. When the Open Championship returned in 1946, who won the tournament?

   A. Johnny Bulla
   B. Sam Snead
   C. Bobby Locke

D. Fred Daly

7. The Vardon Trophy was first awarded based on the lowest scoring average in 1947. Who won it that year?

   A. Jimmy Demaret
   B. Ben Hogan
   C. Sam Snead
   D. Lloyd Mangrum

8. The first Women's U.S. Open took place in which year, with Patty Berg claiming the victory?

   A. 1944
   B. 1945
   C. 1946
   D. 1947

9. The 1949 Open Championship came down to a playoff between a South African player and an Irish player. Who came out on top?

   A. Sid Brews
   B. Bobby Locke
   C. Harry Bradshaw
   D. Christy O'Connor

10. How many major championships did Babe Zaharias win in the 1940s?

    A. Two
    B. Three
    C. Four
    D. Five

11. In 1949, Louise Suggs won the Women's U.S. Open, setting the record for the largest margin of victory. How many strokes did she have between her and the field?

    A. 11
    B. 12
    C. 13
    D. 14

12. In 1945, the Tam O'Shanter Open set the record for the largest purse ever, with how much money?

A. $40,000
B. $50,000
C. $60,000
D. $70,000

13. Jim Ferrier was the first player from which country to win a major championship?

    A. Australia
    B. New Zealand
    C. India
    D. Germany

14. The 1946 U.S. Open needed two playoffs after the players tied through the first 18-hole playoff. Who came out on top?

    A. Byron Nelson
    B. Lloyd Mangrum
    C. Vic Ghezzi
    D. Sam Snead

15. When was the U.S. Junior Amateur first held?

    A. 1944
    B. 1945
    C. 1947
    D. 1948

16. Henry Cotton won his third British Open in 1948. How old was he when he won?

    A. 33
    B. 38
    C. 41
    D. 44

17. In the first Ryder Cup after World War II, the United States crushed Great Britain by scoring how many points out of 12?

    A. 9
    B. 10
    C. 11
    D. 12

18. Ben Hogan won the PGA Championship twice in the 1940s. What year was the second one?

   A. 1944
   B. 1946
   C. 1948
   D. 1949

Chapter 10 Answers:

1. D. Six. From 1940 to 1945, there were no Open Championships. In 1946, the tournament returned.
2. B. Two. He also won it for the third time in 1950, but it was a strong performance from Demaret during the decade.
3. C. 22. It spoke to the strength of the Tour that it was able to expand as the war was taking place in Europe.
4. C. 11. The record still stands to this day. Tiger Woods is second on that list with a streak of seven wins from 2006 to 2007.
5. B. 1945. He won $63,336 that year, and he only won $37,968 in 1944, even though both numbers led the Tour for each year.
6. B. Sam Snead. He won with a score of -2, finishing four strokes ahead of Johnny Bulla and Bobby Locke.
7. A. Jimmy Demaret. His average score of 69.90 was good enough to win the trophy that year.
8. C. 1946. Berg defeated Betty Jameson in the final round, five and four, to win the $5,600 prize.
9. B. Bobby Locke. He defeated Harry Bradshaw in a playoff to capture the title at Royal St George's.
10. D. Five. She was also named the AP Female Athlete of the Year three years in a row.
11. D. 14. Babe Zaharias was closest, but Suggs' -9 for the tournament was plenty good enough to win.
12. C. $60,000. The record would continue to increase over the years, speaking to the popularity and growth of the game.
13. A. Australia. He defeated Chick Harbert two and one to win the 1947 PGA Championship.
14. B. Lloyd Mangrum. He defeated Byron Nelson and Vic Ghezzi in the second playoff after all three players tied the first 18-hole playoff with 72.
15. D. 1948. In the first tournament, Dean Lind defeated Ken Venturi in the final.
16. C. 41. At a time when people didn't necessarily live as long as they do today, it was an impressive feat.
17. C. 11. It was an 11–1 victory that marked the third straight Ryder Cup for the USA.

18. C. 1948. He defeated Mike Turnesa seven and six to claim the championship, though a severe car accident would nearly end his career one year later.

Did You Know?

Ben Hogan lost the 1949 Phoenix Open in a playoff and was in a car accident on the way home from the tournament. He suffered a double fracture of his pelvis, a fractured collar bone, a left ankle fracture, a chipped rib, and blood clots that nearly killed him.

CHAPTER 11: THE 1950S

1. In which year was the Women's Professional Golf Association replaced by the LPGA?

    A. 1950
    B. 1952
    C. 1954
    D. 1955

2. Ben Hogan returned from his car accident to win which major championship in June 1950?

    A. PGA Championship
    B. British Open
    C. U.S. Open
    D. Masters

3. Francis Ouimet made history in 1951 when he became the captain of which group?

    A. U.S. Ryder Cup team
    B. Great Britain Ryder Cup team
    C. R&A
    D. USGA

4. In 1951, the R&A and USGA held a conference to standardize many rules. Which of these could they not agree on?

    A. Eliminating the stymie
    B. Legalizing the center-shafted putter
    C. Ball size
    D. Out-of-bounds penalty of stroke and distance

5. In February 1951, Al Brosch set the PGA record for the lowest round. How low was it?

    A. -8
    B. -10
    C. -11
    D. -12

6. Ben Hogan finished fourth on the PGA Tour Money List in 1951. How many events did he play that year?

    A. Five
    B. Six

C. Seven
   D. Eight

7. How old was Marlene Hagge when she won the Sarasota Open in 1952?

   A. 17 years, 55 days
   B. 18 years, 14 days
   C. 18 years 341 days
   D. 19 years, nine days

8. Who wrote the book *How to Play Your Best Golf All the Time*, which was the first golf book to hit a best-seller list?

   A. Ben Hogan
   B. Lew Worsham
   C. Sam Snead
   D. Tommy Armour

9. Which international team won the first Canada Cup in 1953, which eventually became the World Cup of Golf?

   A. Canada
   B. Argentina
   C. Australia
   D. West Germany

10. Peter Thomson won the Open Championship how many times in a row in the 1950s?

    A. Two
    B. Three
    C. Four
    D. Five

11. Robert Trent Jones, designer of Baltusrol, was receiving complaints that the par-three fourth hole was too hard. What did he shoot when he played it?

    A. Six
    B. Four
    C. One
    D. Three

12. The Great Britain and Ireland team won the 1957 Ryder Cup, their first win since which year?

A. 1937
B. 1935
C. 1933
D. 1939

13. Which player was allowed to take a controversial free drop, helping him save par during the final round of the Masters?

    A. Arnold Palmer
    B. Ken Venturi
    C. Ben Hogan
    D. Gary Player

14. What year saw the first $100,000 purse for a golf tournament?

    A. 1954
    B. 1956
    C. 1958
    D. 1959

15. Ben Hogan fell short of his fifth U.S. Open title when he lost a playoff to which rookie player in 1955?

    A. Jack Fleck
    B. Arnold Palmer
    C. Gary Player
    D. Jack Nicklaus

16. In February 1955, Mike Souchak set a 72-hole record with what score?

    A. -24
    B. -26
    C. -27
    D. -29

17. Which amateur was the first African American to win a golf national championship, which he did in 1959?

    A. Ted Rhodes
    B. Lee Elder
    C. Charlie Sifford
    D. Bill Wright

18. Which player won the 1956 U.S. Open, beating Ben Hogan by one shot?

   A. Ed Furgol
   B. Cary Middlecoff
   C. Julius Boros
   D. Dick Mayer

Chapter 11 Answers:

1. A. 1950. The WPGA had stopped operations in 1949, so the LPGA came in to take over operations.
2. C. U.S. Open. He defeated George Fazio and Lloyd Mangrum in a playoff at Merion Golf Club.
3. C. R&A. Ouimet was the first American to be named captain of the organization.
4. C. Ball size. The two organizations agreed on all of the other rules listed, but they couldn't agree on a standard ball size.
5. C. -11. He set the record during the third round of the Texas Open, at the Breckenridge Park Golf Course in San Antonio.
6. A. Five. Three of those five starts were wins, and the other two were second-place and fourth-place finishes.
7. B. 18 years, 14 days. At the time, it was the record for the youngest player to win an LPGA event.
8. D. Tommy Armour. Armour would also create his own line of golf equipment.
9. B. Argentina. Antonio Cerda and Roberto De Vicenzo teamed up to defeat six other national teams.
10. B. Three. He won in 1954, 1955, and 1956. Bobby Locke won in 1957 before Thomson won again in 1958.
11. C. One. He shot a hole-in-one to prove to the complainants that it was possible to shoot low on the hole.
12. B. 1935. It was a long losing streak, paused briefly by World War II.
13. A. Arnold Palmer. He defeated Doug Ford and Fred Hawkins by one stroke.
14. A. 1954. The Tam O'Shanter World Championship paid $50,000 to Bob Toski, who won first place.
15. A. Jack Fleck. Ben Hogan would not win another major championship in his career.
16. C. -27. His record stood for almost 2,000 PGA Tour events, only broken in 2001 by Mark Calcavecchia.
17. D. Bill Wright. It was an important moment for golf, but the color barrier would not be broken for a few more years.
18. B. Cary Middlecoff. It had been seven years since Middlecoff had last won the U.S. Open, and he would not win it again.

Did You Know?

The 1950s marked the debut of golf on television, including the show called *All-Star Golf*. It was a filmed series of matches that was broadcast on network television.

CHAPTER 12:
THE 1960S

1. Arnold Palmer rallied from how many strokes behind to win the 1960 U.S. Open?

   A. Four
   B. Five
   C. Six
   D. Seven

2. Beginning in what year, players were allowed to lift, clean, and repair ball marks on the green?

   A. 1960
   B. 1961
   C. 1963
   D. 1966

3. Which South African player became the first non-American to win the Masters in 1961?

   A. Jim Ferrier
   B. Gary Player
   C. George Knudson
   D. Bruce Crampton

4. Only a few players have won the U.S. Open as their first professional victory, but which player did it in 1962?

   A. Mickey Wright
   B. Jack Nicklaus
   C. Bob Charles
   D. Dave Marr

5. Painted lines were first used to mark what at the U.S. Open in 1962?

   A. Bunkers
   B. Playable hazards
   C. Out-of-bounds
   D. Water hazards

6. Which player became the first golfer to earn more than $100,000 in one calendar year?

   A. Jack Nicklaus
   B. Gary Player
   C. Arnold Palmer

D. Sam Snead

7. Mickey Wright set the LPGA record in 1963 by winning how many events during the year?

   A. 13
   B. 14
   C. 15
   D. 16

8. In 1963, Bob Charles became the first player from which country to win a major championship?

   A. Australia
   B. Ireland
   C. New Zealand
   D. Austria

9. Tony Lema won which major championship in 1964, just two years before passing away in a plane crash at age 32?

   A. British Open
   B. U.S. Open
   C. PGA Championship
   D. Masters

10. At the 1965 Greater Greensboro Open, Sam Snead won his final event, setting the record at how many Tour victories?

    A. 80
    B. 81
    C. 82
    D. 83

11. Gary Player completed a career "Grand Slam" in 1965 when he won which major championship?

    A. British Open
    B. U.S. Open
    C. PGA Championship
    D. Masters

12. Dave Marr, more known for his great work as a TV commentator, won which major championship in 1965?

    A. British Open

B. U.S. Open
   C. PGA Championship
   D. Masters

13. The PGA Tour's Qualifying School began operations in 1965, with how many players earning their cards in the first year?

    A. 11
    B. 13
    C. 14
    D. 17

14. Which player completed his career "Grand Slam" just one year after Gary Player?

    A. Jack Nicklaus
    B. Arnold Palmer
    C. Lee Trevino
    D. Billy Casper

15. Catherine Lacoste became the first amateur to win the U.S. Women's Open in which year?

    A. 1964
    B. 1965
    C. 1966
    D. 1967

16. Roberto De Vicenzo lost which major championship in 1968 after signing an incorrect scorecard?

    A. British Open
    B. U.S. Open
    C. PGA Championship
    D. Masters

17. "The greatest act of sportsmanship in history" came in 1969, when which player conceded a putt to tie the Ryder Cup?

    A. Arnold Palmer
    B. Jack Nicklaus
    C. Sam Snead
    D. Billy Casper

18. Tony Jacklin won the 1969 British Open, becoming the first British player to win the tournament in how many years?

    A. Eight
    B. 14
    C. 18
    D. 21

Chapter 12 Answers:

1. C. Six. Palmer won the tournament, finishing ahead of Amateur Jack Nicklaus, who finished runner-up.
2. A. 1960. This allowed players to have a better chance to make their putts, no longer worrying about ball marks in their path.
3. B. Gary Player. He would win the tournament twice more but not until 1974 and 1978.
4. B. Jack Nicklaus. It was a grand beginning to what would be a record-setting career.
5. D. Water hazards. Usually, water speaks for itself, but sometimes it can be tricky to tell if a ball is in a hazard or not.
6. C. Arnold Palmer. He would go on to earn much more over his career, and golf was growing with the bigger prizes.
7. A. 13. It was a dominant performance from Wright, which included two major championships.
8. C. New Zealand. He won the 1963 British Open after defeating American Phil Rodgers in a playoff.
9. A. British Open. Lema also finished second at the 1963 Masters.
10. C. 82. The total was nine more than Jack Nicklaus, and the record is one Snead now shares with Tiger Woods, as of 2024.
11. B. U.S. Open. He became only the third player in golf history to accomplish the feat, as Gene Sarazen and Ben Hogan were already on the list.
12. C. PGA Championship. Marr finished two strokes ahead of Billy Casper and Jack Nicklaus.
13. D. 17. There was a total of 49 applicants, as the program was quickly a popular way to join the tour.
14. A. Jack Nicklaus. The feat would not be matched for another 34 years until Tiger Woods joined the list.
15. D. 1967. The feat has not been matched since then.
16. D. Masters. He was tied with Bob Goalby until the penalty dropped him out of first place to end the tournament.
17. B. Jack Nicklaus. The tie was a moment of relief for Great Britain, who had lost the previous five Ryder Cup matches.
18. C. 18. The last British player to win the British Open was Max Faulkner, who won in 1951.

Did You Know?

Charlie Sifford, the first African American Tour member, won his first Tour event at the Greater Hartford Open in 1967.

CHAPTER 13: THE 1970S

1. After finishing as the runner-up in 1969, which player won the 1970 Masters after several years of close calls?

    A. George Archer
    B. Billy Casper
    C. Bob Goalby
    D. Raymond Floyd

2. Which player would be the last European-born player to win the U.S. Open for 40 years, after he accomplished the feat 1970?

    A. Tony Jacklin
    B. David Graham
    C. Ernie Els
    D. Lee Trevino

3. Doug Sanders was one putt away from winning which major in 1970 but instead settled for his fourth major runner-up finish?

    A. U.S. Open
    B. PGA Championship
    C. Masters
    D. British Open

4. In 1971, astronaut Alan Shepard hit a golf ball using which club while on the moon?

    A. Driver
    B. Seven-iron
    C. Six-iron
    D. Pitching wedge

5. Lu Liang-Huan became the first Asian player to finish in the top three of a major tournament at which event in 1971?

    A. U.S. Open
    B. British Open
    C. PGA Championship
    D. Masters

6. In 1972, Carolyn Cudone won the U.S. Senior Women's Amateur again, setting a record for consecutive wins in the event with how many?

    A. Three
    B. Four

C. Five
D. Six

7. When did Spalding introduce the first two-piece ball?

   A. 1972
   B. 1974
   C. 1977
   D. 1978

8. Before turning pro, how many times in a row did Ben Crenshaw win the NCAA title?

   A. One
   B. Two
   C. Three
   D. Four

9. Jack Nicklaus won which major championship in 1973 to break the record for most majors, once held by Bobby Jones?

   A. U.S. Open
   B. British Open
   C. PGA Championship
   D. Masters

10. At 39 years old, how many majors did Gary Player win in 1974?

    A. Zero
    B. One
    C. Two
    D. Three

11. When did The World Golf Hall of Fame open in Pinehurst, North Carolina?

    A. 1973
    B. 1974
    C. 1978
    D. 1980

12. Desmond Muirhead worked with which golfer to design Muirfield Village Golf Club, which opened in 1974?

    A. Arnold Palmer
    B. Lee Trevino

C. Bobby Jones
D. Jack Nicklaus

13. Jack Nicklaus won the first Tournament Players Championship in 1974, finishing two strokes ahead of which player?

    A. Dave Stockton
    B. J.C. Snead
    C. Al Geiberger
    D. Mark Hayes

14. Which of these players was not struck by lightning during the 1975 Western Open?

    A. Jerry Pate
    B. Lee Trevino
    C. Jerry Heard
    D. Bobby Nichols

15. Who received a death threat before deciding to finish and win the 1977 U.S. Open?

    A. Lou Graham
    B. Jerry Pate
    C. Hubert Green
    D. Andy North

16. Which major championship was the first to use the "sudden death" playoff format in 1977?

    A. British Open
    B. U.S. Open
    C. PGA Championship
    D. Masters

17. Which LPGA rookie won five events in a row during the 1978 season?

    A. Chako Higuchi
    B. Donna Caponi
    C. Jane Blalock
    D. Nancy Lopez

18. Which golf equipment company introduced the first metal woods in 1979?

A. Tommy Armour
B. MacGregor
C. Ping
D. Taylor Made

Chapter 13 Answers:

1. B. Billy Casper. He needed a playoff to defeat Gene Littler, after shooting -9 for the tournament.
2. A. Tony Jacklin. He shot -7 for the tournament, seven strokes better than the runner-up, Dave Hill.
3. D. British Open. Sanders missed a short putt on the final hole, forcing a playoff against the eventual winner, Jack Nicklaus.
4. C. Six-iron. Shepard and the NASA crew jokingly called it the "Fra Mauro Country Club."
5. B. British Open. Lee Trevino won that tournament after the two players battled closely in the final round.
6. C. Five. The Carolyn Cudone Intercollegiate Championship is named after her.
7. A. 1972. They called the ball the Top-Flite, which you may recognize as a popular brand today.
8. C. Three. He also won the first PGA Tour he played as a Tour member, the 1973 San Antonio Texas Open.
9. C. PGA Championship. It was Nicklaus' 14th major championship. He also led the Tour Money List again that year.
10. C. Two. Player won the Masters and the British Open, an impressive feat for his age.
11. B. 1974. As of 2009 statistics, it averages about 350,000 visitors every year.
12. D. Jack Nicklaus. There are 36 holes of golf within Muirfield Village, which is also one of the wealthiest neighborhoods in Ohio.
13. B. J.C. Snead. The first TPC was played at the Atlanta Country Club, though it would never be played there again.
14. A. Jerry Pate. The incident caused the PGA to enact new safety standards at PGA Tour events.
15. C. Hubert Green. He finished one stroke ahead of Lou Graham at Southern Hills in Oklahoma.
16. C. PGA Championship. Lanny Wadkins defeated Gene Littler to capture the title at Pebble Beach.
17. D. Nancy Lopez. She would go on to lead the LPGA Tour in scoring and money for that year.
18. D. Taylor Made. The move to metal marked another step forward as technology continued to morph the game.

Did You Know?

The Handicap Research Team of the USGA was formed in 1979. The team would go on to create what is now called the Slope rating system.

CHAPTER 14:
THE 1980S

1. In 1980, which player became the first to win $500,000 in a single season?

   A. Bill Rogers
   B. Johnny Miller
   C. Tom Watson
   D. Fuzzy Zoeller

2. The TPC got a new host course in 1982. What is the name of the course?

   A. Inverrary Country Club
   B. Colonial Country Club
   C. Sawgrass Country Club
   D. TPC Sawgrass Stadium Course

3. In 1981, who became the first woman to earn $1 million in career prize money?

   A. Beth Daniel
   B. Kathy Whitworth
   C. Donna Caponi
   D. Nancy Lopez

4. In 1983, Isao Aoki holed a 128-yard wedge shot on the final hole of which tournament to score an eagle and win?

   A. Hawaiian Open
   B. Phoenix Open
   C. Western Open
   D. Memorial Tournament

5. Which player won his second Masters Tournament in 1983 but couldn't help his Ryder Cup team to victory?

   A. Nick Faldo
   B. Seve Ballesteros
   C. Bernhard Langer
   D. Sam Torrance

6. Ben Crenshaw won the 1984 Masters after how many runner-up finishes in majors?

   A. Two
   B. Three

C. Four
   D. Five

7. How old was Lee Trevino when he won the 1984 PGA Championship?

   A. 41
   B. 44
   C. 45
   D. 49

8. Tom Watson couldn't win the 1984 British Open because which player's birdie on the final hole captured the win?

   A. Lee Trevino
   B. Larry Nelson
   C. Gary Player
   D. Seve Ballesteros

9. In 1985, what did Nancy Lopez shoot to set the new LPGA 72-hole record?

   A. 268
   B. 269
   C. 270
   D. 272

10. Bernhard Langer won which major in 1985, becoming the first German player to win one?

    A. British Open
    B. U.S. Open
    C. PGA Championship
    D. Masters

11. How old was Jack Nicklaus when he won the 1986 Masters?

    A. 44
    B. 45
    C. 46
    D. 47

12. Which was the first PGA Tour tournament to offer a purse of $1 million, in 1986?

    A. Phoenix Open
    B. Greater Greensboro Open

- C. Houston Open
- D. Panasonic Las Vegas Invitational

13. Who made a 40-yard pitch to win the playoff and clinch the 1987 Masters?

    - A. Larry Mize
    - B. Greg Norman
    - C. Nick Faldo
    - D. Larry Nelson

14. Who won his first major championship at the 1987 British Open?

    - A. Larry Nelson
    - B. Lanny Wadkins
    - C. Nick Faldo
    - D. Curtis Strange

15. Which golfer ordered a pizza to protest slow play at the 1989 U.S. Women's Open?

    - A. Linda Hunt
    - B. Lori Garbacz
    - C. Debbie Massey
    - D. Betsy King

16. How much money did Curtis Strange win at the Nabisco Championships at Pebble Beach in 1988, helping him cross $1 million for the year?

    - A. $310,000
    - B. $325,000
    - C. $345,000
    - D. $360,000

17. How many players hit holes-in-one on the same day and hole during the 1989 U.S. Open?

    - A. Two
    - B. Three
    - C. Four
    - D. Five

18. Payne Stewart won which major championship after Mike Reid collapsed in the final round?

A. British Open
B. U.S. Open
C. PGA Championship
D. Masters

Chapter 14 Answers:

1. C. Tom Watson. He won seven events that year and was named the PGA Player of the Year.
2. D. TPC Sawgrass Stadium Course. Though the TPC had used four other courses, the Stadium Course at TPC Sawgrass became the permanent host of the tournament.
3. B. Kathy Whitworth. She won her 81st LPGA Tour event during that season.
4. A. Hawaiian Open. Aoki became the first Japanese player to win on the U.S. Tour.
5. B. Seve Ballesteros. He only won one of his five matches in the Ryder Cup that year.
6. D. Five. Crenshaw had to defeat his friend, Tom Kite, to win his first major championship.
7. B. 44. It was Trevino's sixth major and ten years since his previous major win.
8. D. Seve Ballesteros. When Seve birdied 18, the roar of the crowd happened just as Watson overshot the green on 17.
9. A. 268. Lopez accomplished the feat at the Henredon Classic.
10. D. Masters. Langer, along with Sandy Lyle, helped their Ryder Cup team win in 1985, the first time since 1957.
11. C. 46. He shot a final-round 65 to capture his 18th major title.
12. D. Panasonic Las Vegas Invitational. The other three tournaments listed in the question each offered purses of $500,000.
13. A. Larry Mize. The shot helped Mize defeat Greg Norman, who would not win a tournament for another year.
14. C. Nick Faldo. He played a final round of 18 straight pars to win the title.
15. B. Lori Garbacz. She finished the tournament six shots back, good enough for T-5.
16. D. $360,000. Strange ended the year with $1,147,644. It helped that he also won his first major that year.
17. C. Four. Doug Weaver, Mark Wiebe, Jerry Pate, and Nick Price all holed the par-three sixth hole. None of them won the tournament, though.
18. C. PGA Championship. Stewart was well known on the Tour for his unique style in terms of clothing.

Did You Know?

Square-grooved clubs were banned in 1988, but the manufacturer fought in court to get the ban rescinded two years later.

CHAPTER 15: THE 1990S

1. Shoal Creek GC hosted which major tournament in 1990, causing controversy as the club did not allow Black members?

   A. U.S. Open
   B. British Open
   C. PGA Championship
   D. Masters

2. The R&A finally adopted which ball size in 1990, standardizing the Rules of Golf worldwide?

   A. 43mm
   B. 45mm
   C. 47mm
   D. 49mm

3. In 1990, which tournament was played for the first time in Orlando, Florida, at Lake Nona Golf Club?

   A. Ryder Cup
   B. Solheim Cup
   C. Walker Cup
   D. Presidents Cup

4. John Daly won the PGA Championship in 1991 even though he was in which spot on the list of alternates?

   A. Six
   B. Seven
   C. Eight
   D. Nine

5. In 1991, which amateur player won the PGA Tour's Northern Telecom Open?

   A. Kenny Perry
   B. Larry Silveria
   C. Phil Mickelson
   D. Billy Ray Brown

6. Chip Beck infamously laid up on the 15th hole of the 1993 Masters, allowing which player an easier path to victory?

   A. Phil Mickelson
   B. Bernhard Langer
   C. Payne Stewart
   D. Greg Norman

7. Who won the 1993 LPGA Championship?

    A. Betsy King
    B. Lauri Merten
    C. Patty Sheehan
    D. Brandie Burton

8. Who led the PGA Tour Money List for the second year in a row in 1994?

    A. Greg Norman
    B. Nick Price
    C. Ernie Els
    D. Colin Montgomerie

9. Ernie Els won which major championship in 1994 by surviving a three-way playoff?

    A. British Open
    B. U.S. Open
    C. PGA Championship
    D. Masters

10. Tiger Woods became the youngest player to win which tournament in 1994?

    A. U.S. Open
    B. U.S. Amateur
    C. British Amateur
    D. PGA Championship

11. Which player won the Open Championship in 1995 after defeating Costantino Rossa in a playoff?

    A. John Daly
    B. Phil Mickelson
    C. Tiger Woods
    D. Greg Norman

12. Ben Crenshaw won which major tournament in 1995 just days after the passing of his friend and mentor Harvey Penick?

    A. British Open
    B. U.S. Open
    C. PGA Championship
    D. Masters

13. Who became the youngest ever Masters Champion in 1997?

    A. Phil Mickelson
    B. Tiger Woods
    C. Justin Leonard
    D. Jesper Parnevik

14. Though Tiger Woods led the PGA Tour Money List in 1997, which Senior PGA Tour player earned more?

    A. Hale Irwin
    B. Gil Morgan
    C. Isao Aoki
    D. Jay Sigel

15. How old was Mark O'Meara when he won his first major championship in 1998?

    A. 37
    B. 38
    C. 40
    D. 41

16. Which LPGA player led the Tour's Money List in 1998 with more than $1 million?

    A. Karrie Webb
    B. Donna Andrews
    C. Annika Sorenstam
    D. Se Ri Pak

17. Who came within one shot of winning the 1999 PGA Championship?

    A. Phil Mickelson
    B. Sergio Garcia
    C. Tiger Woods
    D. Ernie Els

18. Which player briefly held the top spot in the world rankings in 1999 but finished the year in second?

    A. Jose Maria Olazabal
    B. Vijay Singh
    C. Justin Leonard
    D. David Duval

Chapter 15 Answers:

1. C. PGA Championship. While Shoal Creek changed its policy, several other country clubs decided to withdraw from the PGA Tour instead of changing their policies.
2. A. 43mm. It only took the R&A 38 years to come around on the ball size issue.
3. B. Solheim Cup. The United States won the inaugural tournament 11.5 to 4.5.
4. D. Nine. Daly got the opportunity to play in the tournament after Nick Price withdrew.
5. C. Phil Mickelson. It was the beginning of a great career for the left-handed player.
6. B. Bernhard Langer. Commentators on the broadcast were vocal about their disagreement with Beck's decision.
7. C. Patty Sheehan. It was her 31st LPGA victory, earning her $150,000 of the $1 million purse.
8. B. Nick Price. He also won two major championships that season.
9. B. U.S. Open. He defeated Colin Montgomerie and Loren Roberts in the playoff to win.
10. B. U.S. Amateur. He was 18 when he won the tournament, taking the record from several players who accomplished the feat at 19, including Jack Nicklaus.
11. A. John Daly. He was happy to prove that his win in 1991 was not just luck.
12. D. Masters. It was his second Masters victory, which he earned by outlasting Davis Love III and Greg Norman.
13. B. Tiger Woods. He was 21 years, three months at the time of his record-setting victory.
14. A. Hale Irwin. Irwin raked in $2.3 million that year, compared to $2.06 for Woods.
15. D. 41. He won the Masters, becoming one of the few champions to birdie the final hole for the win.
16. C. Annika Sorenstam. She led the Money List despite not winning a major tournament.
17. B. Sergio Garcia. He was only 19 at the time but almost caught Tiger Woods, who won his second major.
18. D. David Duval. He won four events before the Masters, including the TPC. He ended up in second place behind Woods.

Did You Know?

The World Golf Championships were played for the first time in 1999. The Match Play Championship was won by Jeff Maggert.

CHAPTER 16:
THE 2000S

1. Tiger Woods dominated the 2000 season, winning how many of the 25 events he entered?

    A. Eight
    B. Ten
    C. 11
    D. 12

2. Who won the LPGA Championship during the 2000 season?

    A. Karrie Webb
    B. Juli Inkster
    C. Annika Sorenstam
    D. Se Ri Pak

3. Which major championship was the final piece in the Tiger Slam?

    A. British Open
    B. U.S. Open
    C. PGA Championship
    D. Masters

4. In 2001, the LPGA added two more major championship events. Who won two majors that year?

    A. Se Ri Pak
    B. Annika Sorenstam
    C. Karrie Webb
    D. Cristie Kerr

5. Which of these players won the four-man playoff to win the 2002 Open Championship?

    A. Thomas Levet
    B. Stuart Appleby
    C. Steve Elkington
    D. Ernie Els

6. Which player held off Tiger Woods to win the 2002 PGA Championship?

    A. Justin Leonard
    B. Rich Beem
    C. Stuart Appleby
    D. Phil Mickelson

7. Who was the first left-handed golfer to win the Masters?

A. Phil Mickelson
   B. Nick O'Hern
   C. Mike Weir
   D. Bubba Watson

8. Who won the 2003 Presidents Cup?

   A. The United States
   B. International team
   C. Tournament was canceled
   D. The teams shared the trophy

9. How old was Michelle Wie when she won the U.S. Women's Amateur Public Links?

   A. 13
   B. 14
   C. 15
   D. 16

10. In 2004, who became the youngest-ever winner of The Players Championship?

    A. Retief Goosen
    B. Tiger Woods
    C. Adam Scott
    D. Todd Hamilton

11. In 2005, Tiger Woods went back and forth with which player for the World Number One ranking?

    A. Phil Mickelson
    B. Vijay Singh
    C. Colin Montgomerie
    D. Retief Goosen

12. Phil Mickelson captured his second major in a row when he won which championship in 2006?

    A. British Open
    B. U.S. Open
    C. PGA Championship
    D. Masters

13. In 2006, which course hosted the Open Championship for the first time since 1967?

A. Royal Liverpool
   B. Carnoustie
   C. Royal Troon
   D. Royal Lytham & St Annes

14. The 2006 PGA Championship was the longest course in major championship history. How long was it?

    A. 7,326 yards
    B. 7,561 yards
    C. 7,604 yards
    D. 7,684 yards

15. Angel Cabrera became which country's first U.S. Open winner in 2007?

    A. Spain
    B. Mexico
    C. Argentina
    D. Brazil

16. Which player won the inaugural FedEx Cup at the end of the 2007 season?

    A. Phil Mickelson
    B. Tiger Woods
    C. Justin Rose
    D. Steve Stricker

17. Tiger Woods needed a birdie on 18 to force a playoff against which player to win the 2008 U.S. Open?

    A. Rocco Mediate
    B. Ernie Els
    C. Sergio Garcia
    D. Stewart Cink

18. Y.E. Yang won which major championship in 2009, catching Tiger Woods on the leaderboard?

    A. British Open
    B. U.S. Open
    C. PGA Championship
    D. Masters

Chapter 16 Answers:

1. C. 11. He won three majors and broke all-time scoring records at each one.
2. B. Juli Inkster. She won by defeating Stefania Croce in a playoff, as both players finished with a score of -3.
3. D. Masters. Tiger Woods became the first player to hold all four major championships at the same time with the victory at the 2001 Masters.
4. C. Karrie Webb. Though Webb won those two majors, it was Sorenstam at the top of the Money List once again.
5. D. Ernie Els. Ernie's third-round 72 was nine shots better than Woods, who struggled in the windy conditions.
6. B. Rich Beem. He finished one shot ahead of Woods, with the rest of the pack four more shots behind.
7. C. Mike Weir. He won the 2003 Masters, which also made him the first Canadian player to win a major championship.
8. D. The teams shared the trophy. With both teams tied, Tiger Woods and Ernie Els ran out of daylight and decided to call it a draw.
9. A. 13. She went on to become the youngest player to make an LPGA cut at the 2003 Kraft Nabisco Championship.
10. C. Adam Scott. He won the tournament by one stroke over Padraig Harrington.
11. B. Vijay Singh. Woods won two majors, but Singh's consistent play through the season kept him close for much of it.
12. D. Masters. Mickelson had also won the 2005 PGA Championship, so it was his third major championship, and second in a row.
13. A. Royal Liverpool. Tiger Woods won the tournament thanks to a 67 in the final round.
14. B. 7,561 yards. Tiger Woods pulled away on the final day of the tournament for his 12th major championship win.
15. C. Argentina. Cabrera won the tournament by one stroke, just ahead of Jim Furyk and Tiger Woods.
16. B. Tiger Woods. He finished eight shots ahead of Mark Calcavecchia and Zach Johnson.
17. A. Rocco Mediate. Woods made par on the first hole to win the playoff and the major championship.
18. C. PGA Championship. Yang also became the first Asian-born player to win a major championship.

Did You Know?

Though Tiger Woods did not win the Tour Championship, his second-place finish in 2009 was good enough for him to capture another FedEx Cup.

CHAPTER 17: THE 2010S

1. In 2010, Graeme McDowell became the first European to win the U.S. Open since which year?

    A. 1960
    B. 1970
    C. 1980
    D. 1990

2. How many strokes did Louis Oosthuizen have as a lead when he won the 2010 Open Championship?

    A. Four
    B. Five
    C. Six
    D. Seven

3. Tim Clark won the 2010 Players Championship, but how many PGA events had he played before getting that first victory?

    A. 181
    B. 192
    C. 206
    D. 217

4. In 2011, how many players won their first major championship?

    A. One
    B. Two
    C. Three
    D. Four

5. Which player became the World Number One after defeating the reigning World Number One at the 2011 BMW PGA Championship?

    A. Luke Donald
    B. Lee Westwood
    C. Martin Kaymer
    D. Tiger Woods

6. Adam Scott finished one stroke back of the winner of the 2012 Open Championship. Which player won?

    A. Rory McIlroy
    B. Ernie Els
    C. Webb Simpson

D. Bubba Watson

7. Though Rory McIlroy was Player of the Year and led the Money List in 2011, who won the FedEx Cup that year?

   A. Steve Stricker
   B. Rory McIlroy
   C. Brandt Snedeker
   D. Justin Rose

8. Who was the first player from mainland U.K. since 1970 to win the U.S. Open?

   A. Adam Scott
   B. Justin Rose
   C. Angel Cabrera
   D. Henrik Stenson

9. Which PGA player won the 2013 FedEx Cup by winning two playoff events?

   A. Adam Scott
   B. Dustin Johnson
   C. Zach Johnson
   D. Henrik Stenson

10. Which player won two majors in 2014 but did not capture the FedEx Cup?

    A. Billy Horschel
    B. Rory McIlroy
    C. Bubba Watson
    D. Martin Kaymer

11. Which player outlasted Rory McIlroy and Jim Furyk to win the Tour Championship and the FedEx Cup in 2014?

    A. Geoff Ogilvy
    B. Bubba Watson
    C. Billy Horschel
    D. Hunter Mahan

12. Who won the 2015 Masters, tying the course record in the process?

    A. Phil Mickelson
    B. Justin Rose
    C. Jordan Spieth

D. Zach Johnson

13. Jason Day set a new major championship record with his final score at the 2015 PGA Championship. What was his score?

    A. -20
    B. -21
    C. -22
    D. -23

14. Which player won the 2015 Players Championship after surviving a three-hole aggregate playoff?

    A. Kevin Kisner
    B. Sergio Garcia
    C. Rickie Fowler
    D. Jason Day

15. Which Englishman won the 2016 Masters, the first English player to win the tournament in 20 years?

    A. Danny Willett
    B. Lee Westwood
    C. Paul Casey
    D. Tyrrell Hatton

16. Which of these major championships did Sergio Garcia first win in 2017?

    A. British Open
    B. U.S. Open
    C. PGA Championship
    D. Masters

17. In 2018, which player won two major championships, including one with Tiger Woods on his heels?

    A. Patrick Reed
    B. Francesco Molinari
    C. Brooks Koepka
    D. Xander Schauffele

18. In 2019, Tiger Woods won his 15th major championship. Which tournament was it?

    A. British Open

B. U.S. Open
C. PGA Championship
D. Masters

Chapter 17 Answers:

1. B. 1970. McDowell won the tournament by one stroke, just ahead of French player Gregory Havret.
2. D. Seven. Lee Westwood was the runner-up, but the final results were not very close.
3. C. 206. Clark had previously won more money than anyone else on Tour who did not have a win.
4. D. Four. Charl Schwartzel, Rory McIlroy, Darren Clarke, and Keegan Bradley all won their first major in 2011.
5. A. Luke Donald. Donald defeated current World Number One Lee Westwood in the first playoff hole to win the title and take the top spot in the world rankings.
6. B. Ernie Els. It was the fourth major championship for Els.
7. C. Brandt Snedeker. He finished three strokes ahead of Justin Rose to win the title.
8. B. Justin Rose. Before Rose's win, Tony Jacklin was the last mainland U.K. player to win the tournament.
9. D. Henrik Stenson. Before his two wins in the FedEx Cup playoffs, he had not won since the 2009 Players Championship.
10. B. Rory McIlroy. He captured the Open Championship and the PGA Championship that year.
11. C. Billy Horschel. He finished three strokes ahead of both players, and his second straight victory carried him to the FedEx Cup.
12. C. Jordan Spieth. His 270 tied a record previously set by Tiger Woods.
13. A. -20. It was the best score at a major championship since Tiger Woods shot -19 at the 2000 British Open.
14. C. Rickie Fowler. He defeated Sergio Garcia and Kevin Kisner in the playoff, though he needed a sudden-death fourth hole to overcome Kisner's bid for victory.
15. A. Danny Willett. The win was Willett's first major championship, and he finished three strokes ahead of Jordan Spieth and Lee Westwood.
16. D. Masters. Garcia needed a playoff to defeat Justin Rose for his first major victory.
17. C. Brooks Koepka. He won the U.S. Open and PGA Championship, the first player to win both those tournaments in the same year since 2000 when Tiger Woods did it.

18. D. Masters. Woods won by one stroke, just ahead of Dustin Johnson, Brooks Koepka, and Xander Schauffele.

Did You Know?

In 2019, Brooks Koepka became the first golfer to simultaneously hold the last two titles of two different majors, as he had won the 2017 and 2018 U.S. Open and the 2018 and 2019 PGA Championships.

CHAPTER 18:
2020 TO 2024

1. In 2020, which major championship was canceled altogether?

    A. British Open
    B. U.S. Open
    C. PGA Championship
    D. Masters

2. Which player won the 2020 PGA Championship, marking his first major victory?

    A. Paul Casey
    B. Collin Morikawa
    C. Dustin Johnson
    D. Matthew Wolff

3. Who was the only player to finish under par at the 2020 U.S. Open?

    A. Matthew Wolff
    B. Brooks Koepka
    C. Bryson DeChambeau
    D. Cameron Smith

4. Though the 2020 Masters was originally scheduled for the month of April, it was held in which month because of the COVID-19 pandemic?

    A. September
    B. October
    C. November
    D. December

5. Hideki Matsuyama became the first Japanese player to win a major when he won which one in 2021?

    A. British Open
    B. U.S. Open
    C. PGA Championship
    D. Masters

6. How old was Phil Mickelson when he won the 2021 PGA Championship?

    A. 50
    B. 51
    C. 52

D. 53

7. Which player won the 2021 FedEx Cup thanks to two victories in the three playoff events?

   A. Bryson DeChambeau
   B. Patrick Cantlay
   C. Tony Finau
   D. Jon Rahm

8. Which LPGA player finished atop the 2021 Money List?

   A. Nelly Korda
   B. Nasa Hataoka
   C. Lydia Ko
   D. Ko Jin-young

9. Which player finished the 2022 Open Championship strong, becoming only the third player to ever card 64 or lower in the final round of the event?

   A. Cameron Young
   B. Scottie Scheffler
   C. Cameron Smith
   D. Justin Thomas

10. In the 2022 Presidents Cup, the U.S. team won by five points. How many times in a row did they win the tournament after that victory?

    A. Nine
    B. Eight
    C. Seven
    D. Six

11. Though Rory McIlroy won the FedEx Cup in 2022, who was atop the Money List?

    A. Patrick Cantlay
    B. Will Zalatoris
    C. Scottie Scheffler
    D. Im Sung-jae

12. The 2023 Ryder Cup was held in which country, where Team Europe was victorious?

    A. United States

B. Italy
C. England
D. Scotland

13. Brooks Koepka won his ninth career tournament in 2023 at which event?

    A. PGA Championship
    B. Wells Fargo Championship
    C. RBC Canadian Open
    D. Travelers Championship

14. How many players on the 2023 PGA Money List Top Ten were not American?

    A. Two
    B. Three
    C. Four
    D. Five

15. Though Scottie Scheffler was atop the 2023 Money List and won Player of the Year, who won the 2023 FedEx Cup?

    A. Jon Rahm
    B. Rory McIlroy
    C. Max Homa
    D. Viktor Hovland

16. In 2024, the prize for winning the FedEx Cup was increased to how much money?

    A. $20 million
    B. $24 million
    C. $25 million
    D. $28 million

17. Who won the PGA Championship and the Open Championship in 2024?

    A. Bryson DeChambeau
    B. Xander Schauffele
    C. Scottie Scheffler
    D. Hideki Matsuyama

18. At the 2024 U.S. Open, who missed two par putts of less than five feet on 16 and 18 to lose by one stroke?
   A. Rory McIlroy
   B. Bryson DeChambeau
   C. Patrick Cantlay
   D. Tony Finau

Chapter 18 Answers:

1. A. British Open. The tournament was canceled due to the COVID-19 pandemic.
2. B. Collin Morikawa. He held a two-stroke lead over Paul Casey and Dustin Johnson.
3. C. Bryson DeChambeau. It was DeChambeau's first major victory, which he won by six strokes.
4. C. November. Dustin Johnson won the tournament by five strokes, earning his second major championship.
5. D. Masters. He finished one stroke ahead of Will Zalatoris to win the title, also making him the first Asian-born player to win that tournament.
6. A. 50. At 50 years and 11 months, Mickelson became the oldest major champion in golf history.
7. B. Patrick Cantlay. He defeated DeChambeau in a playoff at the BMW Championship, then finished one stroke ahead of Rahm at the Tour Championship.
8. D. Ko Jin-young. He finished with $3.5 million in prize money, more than $1 million more than Korda, who was second on the list.
9. C. Cameron Smith. It was Smith's first major championship victory, as well.
10. A. Nine. As of 2024, in the 15 times the tournament has been held, the International Team has only won one time.
11. C. Scottie Scheffler. His $14 million was a new PGA record, one that he would break one year later.
12. B. Italy. Team Europe won the contest 16.5 to 11.5 points, led by team captain Luke Donald.
13. A. PGA Championship. Koepka finished with a two-stroke lead at the Oak Hill Country Club in New York.
14. B. Three. Jon Rahm finished second, Viktor Hovland third, and Rory McIlroy was fourth on the list.
15. D. Viktor Hovland. Hovland's victory at the BMW Championship set him up for victory at the Tour Championship.
16. C. $25 million. It increased by $7 million from the previous year.
17. B. Xander Schauffele. At the PGA, he finished three strokes ahead of Tony Finau, Mark Hubbard, and Sahith Theegala.
18. A. Rory McIlroy. Bryson DeChambeau benefited from the missed putts, winning the major championship, his second U.S. Open.

Did You Know?

Scottie Scheffler won the men's golf event at the 2024 Olympic Games, with Tommy Fleetwood winning silver and Hideki Matsuyama winning bronze.

CHAPTER 19:
The Professional Golfers' Association

1. The Professional Golfers' Association (PGA) of America, the precursor to the PGA, was founded in what year?

    A. 1912
    B. 1916
    C. 1920
    D. 1922

2. How much prize money did Rodman Wanamaker donate to help kickstart what would become the PGA Championship tournament?

    A. $2,000
    B. $2,350
    C. $2,580
    D. $2,690

3. How many members were elected to the PGA of America in April 1916?

    A. 64
    B. 69
    C. 75
    D. 78

4. Which of these was not one of the first PGA Sections when the organization was formed?

    A. Southwestern
    B. Pacific
    C. Southeastern
    D. Middle States

5. The PGA of America had a "Caucasian-only" membership clause until what year, when it was removed from the organization's constitution?

    A. 1955
    B. 1961
    C. 1966
    D. 1969

6. Following a dispute on how to use increased revenues, the PGA Tour broke away from the PGA in what year?

    A. 1966
    B. 1967
    C. 1968

D. 1969

7. As of 2024, the PGA has had 43 presidents. Which PGA Section has had the most presidents?

   A. Metropolitan
   B. Philadelphia
   C. Carolinas
   D. Southern California

8. Who was the last PGA President to serve more than two years?

   A. Max Elbin
   B. Warren Cantrell
   C. Henry Poe
   D. Suzy Whaley

9. The PGA Gallery is located in the PGA Golf Club, in which state?

   A. North Carolina
   B. New York
   C. Florida
   D. California

10. In what year did the Open Championship become a PGA Tour event?

    A. 1916
    B. 1921
    C. 1959
    D. 1995

11. What was the first PGA Tour event named after a golfer?

    A. The Arnold Palmer Invitational
    B. The Bobby Jones Open
    C. The Tommy Armour Championship
    D. The Byron Nelson

12. CBS broadcasted which working-class player's first Masters Tournament win in 1958?

    A. Ben Hogan
    B. Arnold Palmer
    C. Jack Nicklaus
    D. Sam Snead

13. The PGA of America kept control of two important events. Which of them became more popular in 1979?

    A. PGA Championship
    B. Presidents Cup
    C. Ryder Cup
    D. Tour Championship

14. The PGA Tour briefly changed its name in what year, calling themselves the Tournament Players Association Tour?

    A. 1980
    B. 1981
    C. 1983
    D. 1986

15. The PGA Tour and European Tour established the Official World Golf Ranking in which year?

    A. 1984
    B. 1986
    C. 1990
    D. 1993

16. Tim Finchem became the commissioner of the PGA Tour in 1994. How many commissioners had come before him?

    A. One
    B. Two
    C. Three
    D. Four

17. Tiger Woods dominated much of the tour in the 2000s. How many of his 82 wins came from 2000 to 2009?

    A. 34
    B. 46
    C. 57
    D. 68

18. The PGA Tour invented the FedEx Cup because all four majors are completed by which month of the year?

    A. July
    B. August
    C. September
    D. October

Chapter 19 Answers:

1. B. 1916. The Association was established in April of that year after a luncheon in January sparked the idea.
2. C. $2,580. Wanamaker also donated a trophy, which would become the Rodman Wanamaker Trophy, awarded to the winner of the PGA Championship.
3. D. 78. That number includes 35 PGA Charter members, and 28 of them were not from the United States.
4. A. Southwestern. Though the PGA began with seven sections, it has since expanded to 41.
5. B. 1961. The members had voted to keep the clause one year earlier, but they bowed to pressure from California's Attorney General.
6. C. 1968. The two sides reached a compromise after a few months, but it still marked a new beginning for the PGA Tour.
7. D. Southern California. They have had five presidents; Philadelphia and Metropolitan have had four each, and the Carolinas have had three.
8. A. Max Elbin. He served as the PGA President from 1966 to 1968, including the split with the PGA Tour.
9. C. Florida. The PGA Gallery displays golf's major trophies, along with artifacts from PGA history.
10. D. 1995. Though it did not become a PGA Tour event until then, the PGA decided to recognize all previous victories at the event as PGA Tour victories.
11. D. The Byron Nelson. The tournament was first held in 1968, and it has been played every year since then.
12. B. Arnold Palmer. Palmer also won a total of 13 PGA Tour events throughout the decade.
13. C. Ryder Cup. The event was not popular until 1979 when players from continental Europe were allowed to compete, making it more competitive.
14. B. 1981. It all started with a marketing dispute in August of 1981, but they changed their name back in March of 1982.
15. B. 1986. The two organizations could then compete for the best golfers with the worldwide ranking system.
16. B. Two. Finchem served as the commissioner until January 1, 2017.
17. C. 57. His dominance helped the PGA Tour grow in popularity throughout the decade.

18. B. August. The FedEx Cup helps keep fans interested in the rest of the tournament schedule.

Did You Know?

In 2007, the PGA Tour invented the Fall Series, which was a number of events that included a regular season and playoff format for the FedEx Cup.

CHAPTER 20:
The Ladies Professional Golf Association

1. How many players were in the LPGA when it was founded?

    A. Ten
    B. 13
    C. 15
    D. 17

2. In which year was the LPGA founded?

    A. 1950
    B. 1952
    C. 1955
    D. 1958

3. What American city hosted the first official LPGA tournament?

    A. Atlanta
    B. Wichita
    C. Tampa
    D. Albany

4. Who won the first LPGA tournament, shocking the field?

    A. Babe Zaharias
    B. Alice Bauer
    C. Patty Berg
    D. Polly Riley

5. The LPGA hosted its first tournament outside of the USA in which country?

    A. Mexico
    B. Japan
    C. Canada
    D. Cuba

6. How many holes was the Cross Country Weathervane event?

    A. 36
    B. 72
    C. 90
    D. 144

7. How many wins did Babe Zaharias have from officially recognized tournaments before she started winning in the LPGA?

A. Ten
   B. 11
   C. 12
   D. 13

8. Betsy Rawls, a Hall of Fame LPGA player, won her first LPGA event in which year?

   A. 1950
   B. 1951
   C. 1953
   D. 1955

9. Who won the first Vare Trophy, awarded in 1953?

   A. Jackie Pung
   B. Louise Suggs
   C. Patty Berg
   D. Babe Zaharias

10. Fay Crocker became the first LPGA player from outside the USA to win a tournament. Which country was she from?

    A. Canada
    B. Uruguay
    C. England
    D. Scotland

11. Which player won her first LPGA event in 1956, on her way to 82 career wins, second all-time?

    A. Betty Dodd
    B. Kathy Cornelius
    C. Joyce Ziske
    D. Mickey Wright

12. The LPGA Tour first honored a Rookie of the Year in which year?

    A. 1959
    B. 1962
    C. 1965
    D. 1969

13. Four years after Rookie of the Year was introduced, the LPGA Tour recognized their first Player of the Year. Who was it?

A. Kathy Whitworth
B. Mickey Wright
C. Carol Mann
D. Jan Ferraris

14. In 1971, the Sears Women's World Classic was the first LPGA event to have a first prize of how much money?

    A. $7,500
    B. $9,000
    C. $10,000
    D. $20,000

15. The LPGA Tour did not see a left-handed event winner until what year?

    A. 1966
    B. 1970
    C. 1974
    D. 1979

16. Until 2017, which LPGA player was the only woman to win Rookie of the Year and Player of the Year in the same season?

    A. JoAnne Carner
    B. Nancy Lopez
    C. Betsy King
    D. Pat Bradley

17. At the 1979 Women's Kemper Open, how many players participated in the tiebreaking playoff to end the tournament?

    A. Three
    B. Four
    C. Five
    D. Six

18. The Samsung World Championship of Women's Golf was the first LPGA tournament in which country?

    A. China
    B. Malaysia
    C. Japan
    D. South Korea

Chapter 20 Answers:

1. B. 13. It was a small group to start, but it has gained strength in the past couple of decades.
2. A. 1950. It was founded in Wichita, Kansas at the Rolling Hills Country Club.
3. C. Tampa. It was held at the Palma Ceia Golf and Country Club.
4. D. Polly Riley. Although she was an amateur, she was able to come out on top against all the pro women in the field.
5. D. Cuba. The Havana Open was first held in 1956, though it was last held in 1958.
6. D. 144. The event comprised four smaller events, with the combined winner taking home a big money prize. It was a success in bringing early attention to the LPGA.
7. A. Ten. So, when Zaharias won the Titleholders Championship in March of 1950, it was considered her 11th career win.
8. B. 1951. She won the Sacramento Women's Invitational Open on her way to 55 career wins.
9. C. Patty Berg. She would win the trophy twice more in her career.
10. B. Uruguay. Crocker won the Serbin Open in February of 1955 for her first career victory. She would also win the U.S. Women's Open later that year.
11. D. Mickey Wright. She won the 1956 Jacksonville Open to kickstart her career.
12. B. 1962. The first winner was Mary Mills, who would go on to win nine career events, including three majors.
13. A. Kathy Whitworth. It was a meaningful award, as Whitworth would go on to win a total of 88 career events, the most of all-time.
14. C. $10,000. Ruth Jessen won the tournament, and a few months later, Sandra Palmer's first win earned $10,000 at the Sealy LPGA Classic.
15. C. 1974. Bonnie Bryant was the first to do it, and no other LPGA player has done it since.
16. B. Nancy Lopez. The 1978 feat was matched by Sung Hyun Park in 2017, though she split Player of the Year with So Yeon Ryu.
17. C. Five. It was the first time in LPGA history to have that many players in a playoff. It happened again later that season.
18. D. South Korea. Annika Sorenstam won the inaugural event with a -6 score for the tournament.

Did You Know?

The LPGA is the oldest continuing women's professional sports organization in U.S. history.

CHAPTER 21:
LIV GOLF

1. In the name "LIV Golf," what does "LIV" stand for?

    A. Live
    B. 54
    C. Living
    D. Life

2. While plans for a competing league were in talks for many years, LIV Golf held their first tournament in which year?

    A. 2019
    B. 2020
    C. 2021
    D. 2022

3. In the first season of LIV Golf, which player topped the Money List with more than $35 million?

    A. Branden Grace
    B. Peter Uihlein
    C. Dustin Johnson
    D. Talor Gooch

4. Since LIV Golf also has a team format, which team won the first league championship?

    A. 4Aces GC
    B. Crushers GC
    C. Stinger GC
    D. Torque GC

5. Talor Gooch topped the individual points list in 2023. How many of the 14 events did he win?

    A. Three
    B. Four
    C. Five
    D. Six

6. Crushers GC won the 2023 team title. How many of their members finished in the top three of the individual points list?

    A. Zero
    B. One
    C. Two
    D. Three

7. The 2023 LIV Golf season was the first to introduce relegations to the lowest players on the individual points list. How many players to be relegated that year were exempt as team captains?

    A. Zero
    B. Two
    C. Four
    D. Five

8. What happened to LIV Golf's application to join the Official World Golf Ranking system?

    A. Accepted
    B. Rejected
    C. Delayed
    D. Rescinded

9. To join the LIV Golf Tour, beginning in 2023, how many years back can a major champion use their victory to enter the second round of the Promotions Event?

    A. Three
    B. Four
    C. Five
    D. Six

10. Which PGA great was the first CEO of LIV Golf?

    A. Lee Westwood
    B. Phil Mickelson
    C. Jay Monahan
    D. Greg Norman

11. Who took over as CEO of LIV Golf in January 2025?

    A. Scott O'Neil
    B. Jay Monahan
    C. Phil Mickelson
    D. Charl Schwartzel

12. Which player was the first to announce his resignation from the PGA to play in LIV Golf?

    A. Dustin Johnson
    B. Sergio Garcia
    C. Graeme McDowell
    D. Kevin Na

13. Dustin Johnson was supposedly offered $150 million to play in the LIV Golf series. How much had he made as a pro on the PGA Tour before that?

    A. $116 million
    B. $89 million
    C. $74 million
    D. $65 million

14. Which country funded LIV Golf?

    A. India
    B. Saudi Arabia
    C. United Arab Emirates
    D. Qatar

15. There were 14 events during the 2024 LIV Golf League season. How many players tied for most wins at the end of the season?

    A. Zero
    B. Two
    C. Three
    D. Four

16. Which team won the 2024 LIV Golf season?

    A. Crushers GC
    B. Legion XIII
    C. Ripper GC
    D. Smash GC

17. How many trades took place between LIV Golf teams between the 2023 and 2024 seasons?

    A. Zero
    B. One
    C. Two
    D. Three

18. Who was captain of the Ripper GC team during the 2024 LIV Golf season?

    A. Bryson DeChambeau
    B. Jon Rahm
    C. Brooks Koepka
    D. Cameron Smith

Chapter 21 Answers:

1. B. 54. It is named "LIV" because each tournament is 54 holes of play, instead of the 72 holes played on the PGA Tour.
2. D. 2022. The first tournament was the LIV Golf Invitational London, won by Charl Schwartzel.
3. C. Dustin Johnson. He won $10.5 million in individual prize money and $18 million in bonus money.
4. A. 4Aces GC. Talor Gooch, Dustin Johnson, Pat Perez, and Patrick Reed teamed up for the first LIV Golf season victory.
5. A. Three. He finished 22 points ahead of Cameron Smith, and Brooks Koepka finished third.
6. A. Zero. Bryson DeChambeau was the highest-finishing member of the team, and he was fourth on the individual points list.
7. B. Two. Lee Westwood and Martin Kaymer were both exempt from relegation.
8. B. Rejected. The OWGR noted that there were several areas where LIV Golf was not compliant with regulations set by the organization.
9. C. Five. In 2023, any player who won a major championship since 2018 would be entered into the second round of the Promotions Event.
10. D. Greg Norman. He served as the CEO of LIV Golf until January 15, 2025.
11. A. Scott O'Neil. O'Neil is a businessman who did not play professional golf but was once the CEO of the Philadelphia 76ers.
12. D. Kevin Na. He announced his resignation on June 4, 2022, just a few days before announcements from the rest of the players.
13. C. $74 million. That means he made more money by joining LIV Golf than he did by winning 24 PGA Tour events and being a World Number One.
14. B. Saudi Arabia. There was a lot of controversy about the source of the money, as the country has been criticized in the past for human rights issues.
15. C. Three. Brooks Koepka, Joaquin Niemann, and Jon Rahm each won two games.
16. C. Ripper GC. The team was third on the team points list but won the Team Championship at the end of the season.

17. C. Two. Smash GC acquired Talor Gooch for Matthew Wolff, who was sent to RangeGoats GC, and RangeGoats GC also sent Harold Varner III to 4Aces GC for Peter Uihlein.
18. D. Cameron Smith. Neither Smith nor any of his teammates made the top five in individual points or money made, yet the team won the title at the end of the season, winning $50 million.

Did You Know?

LIV Golf allegedly offered Tiger Woods between $700 and $800 million to join their league, but he declined, noting his loyalty to the PGA Tour.

CHAPTER 22:
Senior Professional Golf

1. How old does a golfer need to be if they want to play on the PGA Tour Champions?

    A. 40
    B. 45
    C. 50
    D. 55

2. What year was the PGA Tour Champions founded?

    A. 1937
    B. 1957
    C. 1978
    D. 1980

3. Who has won the most Money List titles in the PGA Tour Champions?

    A. Steven Alker
    B. Bernhard Langer
    C. Jay Haas
    D. Hale Irwin

4. Of all the PGA Tour Champions players, Bernhard Langer has the most tournament wins. How many did he win?

    A. 47
    B. 44
    C. 41
    D. 39

5. In what year did the PGA Tour Champions vote to allow players the use of golf carts for most tournaments?

    A. 2002
    B. 2004
    C. 2006
    D. 2008

6. Though the PGA Tour Champions was founded much later, when was the Senior PGA Championship established?

    A. 1920
    B. 1925
    C. 1933
    D. 1937

7. Who has won the Senior PGA Championship more than any other player?

    A. Hale Irwin
    B. Bernhard Langer
    C. Sam Snead
    D. Gary Player

8. Who did Steve Stricker defeat in a playoff to win the 2023 Senior PGA Championship?

    A. Richard Green
    B. Richard Bland
    C. Stephen Ames
    D. Padraig Harrington

9. What is the highest first round by a PGA Tour Champions player who still went on to win the event?

    A. 74
    B. 77
    C. 79
    D. 80

10. Who was the first Senior PGA Tour player to win Rookie of the Year when it was first awarded in 1990?

    A. Lee Trevino
    B. Chi-Chi Rodriguez
    C. Mike Hill
    D. Jack Nicklaus

11. Since 2016, the Senior Tour has used a format similar to the FedEx Cup to determine the winner of which cup?

    A. Byron Nelson Cup
    B. Tour Champions Cup
    C. Charles Schwab Cup
    D. Senior Tour Cup

12. These four players are the only ones to ever shoot a 60 to open a tournament and then go on to win it. Who did it most recently?

    A. Bruce Fleisher
    B. Michael Allen

C. Nick Price
D. Tom Purtzer

13. Bob Brue holds the record for fewest putts in one round of a Senior PGA Tour event. How many putts is his record?

    A. 19
    B. 18
    C. 17
    D. 16

14. Fred Couples holds the Champions Tour record for best scoring average. What year did he set the record?

    A. 2008
    B. 2010
    C. 2011
    D. 2012

15. Two players have shot -27 at a Champions Tour event. Who did it first?

    A. Padraig Harrington
    B. Bernhard Langer
    C. Arnold Palmer
    D. Jack Nicklaus

16. How many players have shot a 59 during a round on the Tour Champions circuit?

    A. One
    B. Two
    C. Three
    D. Four

17. Padraig Harrington holds the Champions Tour record for lowest stroke total during a 72-hole event. How low did he shoot?

    A. 259
    B. 258
    C. 257
    D. 256

18. Which player is the only one to win four Champions Tour events in a row?

A. Bruce Fleisher
B. Chi-Chi Rodriguez
C. Bernhard Langer
D. Hale Irwin

Chapter 22 Answers:

1. C. 50. Players younger than 50 have to wait until they reach that milestone before joining the senior group.
2. D. 1980. Though the tour was established in 1980, it would not get its current name for many more years.
3. B. Bernhard Langer. He has won 11 Money List titles, including seven in a row from 2012 to 2018.
4. A. 47. He's also the only PGA Tour Champions player to win a tournament by 13 strokes, which he did in 2014 at the Senior Open Championship.
5. C. 2006. However, the players could not use them at major championships and a few other events.
6. D. 1937. It was first played at Augusta National, but it has been most recently and most often played at The Golf Club of Harbor Shores, in Benton Harbor, Michigan, as of 2024.
7. C. Sam Snead. He won the tournament six times in his senior career, while Irwin is second on the list with four wins.
8. D. Padraig Harrington. Stricker won $630,000 for the victory, the first time in the tournament's history that the winner won more than $600,000.
9. B. 77. Hale Irwin had a rough start at the 1998 U.S. Senior Open, but he would finish +1 on the tournament, one shot ahead of Vicente Fernandez.
10. A. Lee Trevino. In his first year on the Senior PGA Tour, Trevino won seven times, most of any player that year.
11. C. Charles Schwab Cup. Bernhard Langer won the title in its first year using the new format.
12. B. Michael Allen. He shot a 60 in the first round of the 2014 Allianz Championship, which he went on to win.
13. C. 17. Brue putted 17 times during the second round of the 1994 Kroger Senior Classic. Notably, he did not win the event.
14. B. 2010. His scoring average that year was 67.96, an incredible season.
15. D. Jack Nicklaus. Back in 1990, he won the 1990 Mazda Senior Tournament Players Championship. Harrington did it in 2022.
16. A. One. Kevin Sutherland. He shot 59 during the second round of the 2014 Dick's Sporting Goods Open. He did not win the tournament.

17. C. 257. Even better, he did it during the 2022 Charles Schwab Cup Championship.
18. B. Chi-Chi Rodriguez. He won four events in a row during the 1987 season.

Did You Know?

Though Bernhard Langer leads in all-time wins for Senior events, Peter Thomson and Hale Irwin are the only players to ever win nine times in one year. Irwin did it in 1997, and Thomson did it in 1985.

CHAPTER 23:
Major Champions

1. Which American golfer won the 1946 British Open but lost money on the trip?

    A. Ben Hogan
    B. Sam Snead
    C. Arnold Palmer
    D. Byron Nelson

2. Pittsburgh writer Bob Drum had a discussion with which golfer, leading to the concept of the modern golf Grand Slam?

    A. Jack Nicklaus
    B. Arnold Palmer
    C. Bobby Jones
    D. Sam Snead

3. When a player wins a major championship, how many years of major championships are they automatically invited to?

    A. Three
    B. Four
    C. Five
    D. Six

4. Only one of the major championships is played at the same course every year. Which one is it?

    A. British Open
    B. U.S. Open
    C. PGA Championship
    D. Masters

5. Which of the four major championships is the only one to invite 20 club professionals who are non-tour regulars to compete?

    A. British Open
    B. U.S. Open
    C. PGA Championship
    D. Masters

6. Which of the four major championships allows the fewest number of players to make the 36-hole cut?

    A. British Open
    B. U.S. Open

    C. PGA Championship
    D. Masters

7. The 2017 U.S. Open was the first to be held on a par-72 course since what year?

    A. 2001
    B. 1997
    C. 1992
    D. 1989

8. The Claret Jug is associated with which of the major championships?

    A. British Open
    B. U.S. Open
    C. PGA Championship
    D. Masters

9. Of the four major championships, which one has produced the lowest score by a player to win the tournament?

    A. British Open
    B. U.S. Open
    C. PGA Championship
    D. Masters

10. Who has the lowest score at a U.S. Open?

    A. Dustin Johnson
    B. Bryson DeChambeau
    C. Rory McIlroy
    D. Henrik Stenson

11. Who has the largest margin of victory at any major championship?

    A. Old Tom Morris
    B. Young Tom Morris
    C. Jack Nicklaus
    D. Tiger Woods

12. The lowest round in a major championship is a 62, but which player is the only one to have done it more than once?

    A. Branden Grace
    B. Xander Schauffele
    C. Rickie Fowler

D. Shane Lowry

13. Who is the only player to win the PGA Championship four years in a row?

    A. Bobby Jones
    B. Sam Snead
    C. Ben Hogan
    D. Walter Hagen

14. Tiger Woods was one major away from the Grand Slam in 2000. What place did he finish the 2000 Masters Tournament?

    A. Third
    B. Fourth
    C. Fifth
    D. Sixth

15. As of 2024, who was the last golfer to win two major championships in a row?

    A. Jordan Spieth
    B. Rory McIlroy
    C. Padraig Harrington
    D. Tiger Woods

16. Everyone knows who has won the most majors, with Jack Nicklaus at the top of the list, but who has more major championship runner-up finishes than any other player?

    A. Phil Mickelson
    B. Jack Nicklaus
    C. Arnold Palmer
    D. Sam Snead

17. Phil Mickelson fell short of the career Grand Slam, never winning the U.S. Open. How many times did he finish as the runner-up?

    A. Four
    B. Five
    C. Six
    D. Seven

18. Besides Craig Wood, who played in the 1930s, who is the only other player to have lost in a playoff at each major championship?

A. Tom Watson
B. Colin Montgomerie
C. Tiger Woods
D. Greg Norman

Chapter 23 Answers:

1. B. Sam Snead. Because the British Open did not have a big purse at the time, Snead returned to the U.S. with $600 less than when he left, despite winning the tournament.
2. B. Arnold Palmer. Certain tournaments came in and out of the rotation as the idea of major tournaments continued to develop.
3. C. Five. The automatic invitations give winners a chance to continue their winning ways.
4. D. Masters. Every year, it is played at Augusta National. Every other major championship has multiple courses that can play host.
5. C. PGA Championship. The tournament is also the only one to invite winners of any PGA Tour event in the year preceding the tournament.
6. D. Masters. The Masters Tournament only allows the top 50 scores and ties to make the cut. The U.S. Open cuts at the top 60, and the other two cut at the top 70.
7. C. 1992. While the tournament is sometimes played on par-71 courses, it is typically played on par-70 courses.
8. A. British Open. The Claret Jug has a history that dates back to 1872.
9. C. PGA Championship. In 2024, Xander Schauffele won the tournament with a -21, the lowest of any major championship.
10. C. Rory McIlroy. He shot a 268 to win the 2011 U.S. Open, which was 16 under par.
11. D. Tiger Woods. He won the 2000 U.S. Open with 15 shots to spare. Old Tom Morris and Young Tom Morris are second and third on the list.
12. B. Xander Schauffele. He shot 62 at the 2023 U.S. Open and the 2024 PGA Championship.
13. D. Walter Hagen. From 1924 to 1927, Hagen was the untouchable champion of that tournament.
14. C. Fifth. Woods would go on to win the next four majors, including the 2001 Masters.
15. A. Jordan Spieth. He won the 2015 Masters and the 2015 U.S. Open.
16. B. Jack Nicklaus. He had 19 runner-up finishes. Seven of those were at the British Open.
17. C. Six. Mickelson's six runner-up finishes at the U.S. Open is more than any other player in history.

18. D. Greg Norman. He also collected a total of eight runner-up finishes at major championships.

Did You Know?

Colin Montgomerie is the only player in golf history to finish runner-up at a major championship five times without ever winning a major.

CHAPTER 24:
The Ryder Cup

1. Which U.S. state hosted the first Ryder Cup in 1927?

   A. New York
   B. Massachusetts
   C. Florida
   D. Georgia

2. Home-field advantage can be important in other sports, but how many times in a row did the home team win the Ryder Cup, beginning with the inaugural tournament in 1927?

   A. Five
   B. Six
   C. Seven
   D. Eight

3. Due to dominance by the United States, when did Great Britain expand to include golfers from continental Europe?

   A. 1971
   B. 1975
   C. 1979
   D. 1983

4. Since 1979, how many times, as of 2024, has Team Europe won the Ryder Cup on foreign soil?

   A. One
   B. Two
   C. Three
   D. Four

5. By comparison, how many times has the United States won the Ryder Cup on foreign soil since 1979?

   A. Zero
   B. One
   C. Two
   D. Three

6. In the ten Ryder Cups from 1995 to 2014, how many did Team Europe win?

   A. Seven
   B. Eight

C. Nine
D. Ten

7. How much prize money was at stake for the 2023 Ryder Cup in Italy?

    A. None
    B. $10 million
    C. $25 million
    D. $40 million

8. When did the Ryder Cup switch from being held on odd years to even years?

    A. 1996
    B. 1998
    C. 2000
    D. 2002

9. After switching to even years for a while, the Ryder Cup switched back to odd years in which year?

    A. 2017
    B. 2019
    C. 2021
    D. 2023

10. How many players comprise a Ryder Cup team?

    A. Eight
    B. Ten
    C. 12
    D. 14

11. How many days does the Ryder Cup span?

    A. Two
    B. Three
    C. Four
    D. Five

12. What is the maximum number of matches one player can participate in during a Ryder Cup tournament?

    A. Six
    B. Five

- C. Four
- D. Three

13. Who showed great sportsmanship by conceding a putt to Tony Jacklin on the final hole of the Ryder Cup, leaving the match a draw?

    - A. Jack Nicklaus
    - B. Arnold Palmer
    - C. Sam Snead
    - D. Tommy Aaron

14. Which player infamously disputed Seve Ballesteros' desire to change his scuffed ball during play at the 1989 Ryder Cup?

    - A. Raymond Floyd
    - B. Mark Calcavecchia
    - C. Fred Couples
    - D. Paul Azinger

15. Who missed the decisive six-foot par putt to lose the 1991 Ryder Cup?

    - A. Seve Ballesteros
    - B. Jose Maria Olazabal
    - C. Nick Faldo
    - D. Bernhard Langer

16. How many points behind were the Americans going into the final day of the 1999 Ryder Cup?

    - A. 4
    - B. 3.5
    - C. 3
    - D. 2.5

17. Which player made the winning putt at the 2012 Miracle at Medinah?

    - A. Rory McIlroy
    - B. Martin Kaymer
    - C. Ian Poulter
    - D. Jason Dufner

18. As of 2024, out of 44 matches, how many times has the United States won the Ryder Cup?

A. 22
B. 25
C. 27
D. 30

Chapter 24 Answers:

1. B. Massachusetts. It was held at the Worcester Country Club, and the home team won the first contest.
2. A. Five. It was not until the Sixth Ryder Cup that the United States was able to win in Great Britain.
3. C. 1979. It also helped that Spanish players like Seve Ballesteros were experiencing success on the Tour at the time.
4. D. Four. They won in 1987, 1995, 2004, and 2012, all in the United States.
5. C. Two. They won in 1981 and 1993. European players on the team shifted the balance of power away from the American team.
6. B. Eight. Since 1979, they have a winning record of 12 wins, nine losses, and one draw.
7. A. None. Along with the Presidents Cup and Solheim Cup, players do not receive prize money. These are among the very few exceptions in professional sports, where players do not win money despite the events making a lot of money.
8. D. 2002. The 2001 event was canceled due to the 9/11 terrorist attack on the United States.
9. C. 2021. The 2020 event was postponed by the COVID-19 pandemic.
10. C. 12. However, those 12 players do not play an equal number of matches during the tournament.
11. B. Three. Day One and Day Two have morning and afternoon matches, while Day Three has only one set of matches.
12. B. Five. The number used to be six, back before the format was adjusted in 1975.
13. A. Jack Nicklaus. He told Tony Jacklin that he thought Jacklin would have made the two-foot putt, but that he wouldn't give him the chance to miss it.
14. D. Paul Azinger. The 1989 Ryder Cup ended in a draw, meaning that Team Europe kept the trophy.
15. D. Bernhard Langer. The War on the Shore was won by the American team, who had not won the Ryder Cup since 1983.
16. A. 4. The American team came back to win the event by a full point, beating the European team by five points in the singles matches.
17. B. Martin Kaymer. The European team had been trailing 2–4 at one moment in the tournament, but they came back to win.

18. C. 27. However, since Team Europe came around, the American team has lost more Ryder Cups than it has won.

Did You Know?

As of 2024, no player has made more appearances in Ryder Cup competitions than Phil Mickelson. His 12 appearances from 1995 to 2018 put him at the top of the list.

CHAPTER 25:
Golf at the Olympics

1. Since 1900, how many times has golf been played at the Summer Olympics?

    A. Two
    B. Three
    C. Four
    D. Five

2. How many Olympic tournaments were attempted but canceled before 1930?

    A. One
    B. Two
    C. Three
    D. Four

3. How many of the top players in the World Golf Ranking automatically qualify for the Olympics?

    A. Ten
    B. 15
    C. 20
    D. 25

4. As of 2024, how many medals has the United States collected between both men's and women's competitions?

    A. 14
    B. 12
    C. Ten
    D. Nine

5. As of 2024, where is Great Britain on the table in terms of total medals for men and women competitors at the Olympics?

    A. Second
    B. Third
    C. Fourth
    D. Fifth

6. At the very first Olympics in 1900, how many competitors took part in the tournament?

    A. Eight
    B. Ten

C. 12
D. 15

7. On the women's side, how many different nations were represented at the 1900 Olympics?

   A. Two
   B. Three
   C. Four
   D. Five

8. In contrast, how many countries were represented at the men's golf competition during the 2016 Summer Olympics?

   A. 24
   B. 27
   C. 31
   D. 34

9. Which woman won the 2016 Summer Olympics gold medal in golf?

   A. Lydia Ko
   B. Shanshan Feng
   C. Inbee Park
   D. Stacy Lewis

10. In Japan for the 2020 Summer Olympics, which country's participant went home with the silver medal in the men's golf competition?

    A. United States
    B. Slovakia
    C. Chinese Taipei
    D. South Korea

11. Nelly Korda's second round in the 2020 Summer Olympics women's golf tournament was the lowest by any player in that competition. What did she shoot?

    A. 66
    B. 64
    C. 62
    D. 60

12. The 2020 women's golf competition needed a sudden-death playoff for the silver medal. Who came out on top?

A. Mone Inami
B. Lydia Ko
C. Aditi Ashok
D. Hannah Green

13. Celine Boutier started the 2024 Summer Olympics with a three-shot lead after the first round. Where did she finish the tournament?

    A. T8
    B. T13
    C. T18
    D. T22

14. By winning the 2024 gold medal, which woman also earned her automatic qualification into the LPGA Hall of Fame?

    A. Esther Henseleit
    B. Lin Xiyu
    C. Amy Yang
    D. Lydia Ko

15. For the men's golf at the 2024 Olympics, how many strokes of a lead did Scottie Scheffler have when the tournament came to a finish?

    A. One
    B. Two
    C. Three
    D. Four

16. Xander Schauffele was second after the first round of the 2024 Olympic tournament and T1 at the end of the second and third rounds. Where did he finish?

    A. Fourth
    B. T5
    C. 8
    D. T9

17. As of 2024, which California course is planned for use in the 2028 Summer Olympics?

    A. Pebble Beach Golf Links
    B. Riviera Country Club
    C. PGA WEST

D. Torrey Pines Golf Course

18. There has only been one team golf competition at the Summer Olympics. What year was that competition held?

    A. 1900
    B. 1904
    C. 2016
    D. 2020

Chapter 25 Answers:

1. D. Five. It was played twice in the early 1900s, but then it was not played until 2016.
2. C. Three. In 1908, it was canceled two days before it was to start. In 1920, two tournaments were canceled due to a lack of competitors.
3. B. 15. However, there is a limit of four players per country.
4. A. 14. The United States players have six gold, three silver, and five bronze across all Olympic competitions.
5. B. Second. They have four total medals, just one ahead of New Zealand on the total medal table.
6. C. 12. The 12 competitors were only from four different countries, and Charles Sands of the USA won gold.
7. A. Two. Only the USA and France were represented, and the USA women swept the medals.
8. D. 34. The three medalists were each from a different country, as well.
9. C. Inbee Park. She won the gold medal with five strokes to spare over Lydia Ko.
10. B. Slovakia. Rory Sabbatini took home the silver medal, finishing one stroke behind Xander Schauffele of the United States.
11. C. 62. Though it was a very low round, she had to hang on to win the gold medal by just one stroke.
12. A. Mone Inami. Inami, playing in her home country of Japan, overcame Lydia Ko to capture the silver medal.
13. C. T18. Boutier shot a 286 for the tournament, eight shots off the lead.
14. D. Lydia Ko. She shot a 278 for the tournament, earning the final point needed for Hall of Fame auto qualification.
15. A. One. Scheffler finished one stroke ahead of Tommy Fleetwood, who finished one stroke ahead of Hideki Matsuyama.
16. D. T9. He shot a 73 on the final day, putting him seven strokes off the lead.
17. B. Riviera Country Club. However, plans may change as the course is located in the Pacific Palisades, near where a large fire ravaged much of the area in early 2025.
18. B. 1904. The United States won all three medals with three different teams of ten players each.

Did You Know?

As of 2025, the 2032 Summer Olympics in Brisbane are set to have the golf tournaments at the Royal Queensland Golf Club.

CHAPTER 26:
The Old Course at St Andrews

1. What year was the Old Course established?
   A. 1552
   B. 1652
   C. 1752
   D. 1852

2. What year did the Old Course get its name?
   A. 1553
   B. 1653
   C. 1795
   D. 1895

3. The Society of St Andrews Golfers was founded in 1754 by a group of how many noblemen, professors, and landowners?
   A. 16
   B. 18
   C. 20
   D. 22

4. St Andrews Links went bankrupt in what year, almost leading to the loss of the golf course?
   A. 1765
   B. 1779
   C. 1785
   D. 1797

5. James Cheape of Strathtyrum officially saved the course from bankruptcy in 1821, buying the land to save it from people using it for what?
   A. Cattle farming
   B. Rabbit farming
   C. Horse farming
   D. Sheep farming

6. Old Tom Morris, who was one of the first great golfers, helped design which holes on the course?
   A. One and 18
   B. Two and 17
   C. Three and 16
   D. Four and 15

7. In the 1750s, the Old Course had 22 holes. When did that number get reduced to 18?

    A. 1761
    B. 1764
    C. 1769
    D. 1777

8. Though the Old Course had 18 holes in the 1860s, Old Tom Morris changed some of the green layouts. How many greens did the course have when he was done?

    A. 18
    B. 15
    C. 13
    D. 11

9. As of 2024, how many times has the Old Course hosted the Open Championship?

    A. 30
    B. 29
    C. 28
    D. 27

10. In the 1921 Open Championship, Bobby Jones infamously got his ball stuck in which hole's bunker and didn't turn in his scorecard?

    A. Eight
    B. 11
    C. 13
    D. 16

11. Bobby Jones became the first amateur to win the Open Championship wire-to-wire. What was his aggregate score in that 1927 tournament?

    A. 281
    B. 284
    C. 285
    D. 289

12. Bobby Jones continued his revenge tour in 1930 when he won the British Amateur by what margin?

A. Six and five
B. Seven and six
C. Eight and seven
D. Nine and eight

13. The town of St Andrews gave Bobby Jones the key to the city in 1958. Jones was the second American to receive it. Who was the first?

    A. George Washington
    B. Benjamin Franklin
    C. Thomas Edison
    D. John Quincy Adams

14. How many bunkers does the Old Course have?

    A. 76
    B. 93
    C. 105
    D. 112

15. The front nine holes have white flags, and the back nine holes have red flags, except for which hole that also has a white flag?

    A. Ten
    B. 14
    C. 15
    D. 18

16. Which of these holes on the Old Course does not have its own, dedicated green?

    A. One
    B. Ten
    C. 17
    D. 18

17. Many of the hazards on the Old Course have names. Which hole features the Valley of Sin?

    A. 15
    B. 16
    C. 17
    D. 18

18. In honor of Bobby Jones, the Old Course named which hole after him?

    A. Three
    B. Six
    C. Nine
    D. Ten

Chapter 26 Answers:

1. A. 1552. While it was established as a golf course that long ago, it would not be called the Old Course for a few hundred years.
2. D. 1895. It was originally known as the "golfing grounds" of St Andrews.
3. D. 22. The society would eventually morph into the R&A, which now governs golf around the world, except in the USA and Mexico.
4. D. 1797. Thankfully, the course was eventually able to recover, though it took 20 years.
5. B. Rabbit farming. The feud between golfers and rabbit farmers was fierce, but golf won out in the end.
6. A. One and 18. Back then, fairways were shared and used in both directions, meaning players would be hitting past each other.
7. B. 1764. William St Clair of Roslin authorized those changes, merging the first four and last four holes into two holes each.
8. D. 11. This is the current layout of the course, with seven double greens and four single greens.
9. A. 30. The Old Course has hosted the Open Championship more than any other course.
10. B. 11. He tried four times but still couldn't get it out, and though he was disqualified for not turning in the scorecard, he still played the fourth round.
11. C. 285. His -7 score was the lowest of any U.S. Open or Open Championship at that time.
12. B. Seven and six. It was a dominant performance by Jones, who would go on to win the other three major championships that year, completing the Grand Slam.
13. B. Benjamin Franklin. Franklin received the key in 1759. Jones was grateful for the honor.
14. D. 112. The last time a bunker was filled in was in 1949 when they filled the Hull bunker on the 15th fairway.
15. D. 18. The 18th flag is white so it can be seen against the background, which is the red Hamilton Grand building.
16. B. Ten. The first, ninth, 17th, and 18th holes all have their own dedicated greens. No sharing.
17. D. 18. It is an eight-foot-deep depression along the front before the 18th green.

18. D. Ten. It is a 386-yard par-four, and it was yet another honor given to Jones for his incredible play and contributions to golf.

Did You Know?

As of 2024, the Women's British Open has been played at the Old Course three times. Lydia Ko is the most recent winner in 2024 with a -7 score total.

CHAPTER 27:
Augusta National Golf Club

1. Augusta National opened in 1932, but when did it host the first Masters Tournament?

    A. 1932
    B. 1933
    C. 1934
    D. 1935

2. The Great Depression caused the owners of Augusta National to scrap many plans. Which of these was not one of them?

    A. Ladies' course
    B. Squash courts
    C. Tennis courts
    D. Baseball field

3. Ed Dudley was the first club pro at Augusta. How many PGA Tour events did he win in his career?

    A. Zero
    B. One
    C. Ten
    D. 15

4. In 1948, which soon-to-be President of the United States enjoyed his visit and became a member of the golf club?

    A. Harry S. Truman
    B. Dwight D. Eisenhower
    C. John F. Kennedy
    D. Lyndon B. Johnson

5. Nick Price set the course record in 1986 with a 63. Who tied the record ten years later?

    A. Greg Norman
    B. Nick Faldo
    C. Phil Mickelson
    D. David Frost

6. Augusta National is well known for its appearance. Which of these actions do they take to control the ambiance?

    A. Import birds to the course
    B. Dye the leaves on the trees

C. Play bird sounds on hidden speakers
   D. Use home-grown pine needles

7. Players who win the Masters Tournament are presented with what color jacket at the Butler Cabin?

   A. Gold
   B. Green
   C. Blue
   D. Red

8. Because of the course's former use, each hole is named after what?

   A. Great players
   B. Former leaders
   C. Geographical locations
   D. Plants or trees

9. Architect Perry Maxwell changed which hole in 1937, transforming it into one of the toughest holes in Masters Tournament history?

   A. Tenth
   B. First
   C. Third
   D. Eighth

10. Amen Corner is the nickname for which holes on the course?

    A. 10–12
    B. 11–13
    C. 12–14
    D. 9–11

11. One famous moment from Amen Corner came in 2016 when which player quadruple bogeyed 12 during the final round, costing him the championship?

    A. Tiger Woods
    B. Phil Mickelson
    C. Jordan Spieth
    D. Rory McIlroy

12. For decades, there was a tree named after President Eisenhower on which hole of Augusta National?

    A. 14th

B. 15th
   C. 16th
   D. 17th

13. Many of the bridges on the course are named after players. Which bridge was the first to be named for a player?

   A. Hogan Bridge
   B. Sarazen Bridge
   C. Nelson Bridge
   D. Rae's Bridge

14. As of 2024, how many chairmen have served Augusta National Golf Club?

   A. Six
   B. Seven
   C. Eight
   D. Nine

15. In what year did Augusta National Golf Club first extend memberships to women?

   A. 2002
   B. 2005
   C. 2009
   D. 2012

16. In 2019, Augusta National established a Women's Amateur tournament that featured how many holes of play?

   A. 18
   B. 36
   C. 54
   D. 72

17. In which year did Augusta National begin awarding green jackets for a Masters Tournament victory?

   A. 1944
   B. 1949
   C. 1954
   D. 1957

18. Only two green jackets have been permanently removed from the course. One belonged to Henry Picard. Who owns the other one?
    A. Jack Nicklaus
    B. Billy Casper
    C. Gary Player
    D. Tom Watson

Chapter 27 Answers:

1. C. 1934. In an attempt to attract both crowds and players, co-founder Clifford Roberts convinced the retired Bobby Jones to participate in the first Masters Tournament.
2. D. Baseball field. Despite plans for a ladies' course, women would not be permitted at Augusta National for quite a long time.
3. D. 15. He was one of the best tour pros of his era.
4. B. Dwight D. Eisenhower. He would visit Augusta 29 times during the course of his presidency.
5. A. Greg Norman. He shot 63 in the first round of the 1996 Masters Tournament but would collapse in the final round, losing to Nick Faldo by five shots.
6. C. Play bird sounds on hidden speakers. They also import pine needles, and they used to dye their ponds blue to make them more appealing to the eye.
7. B. Green. Players who win multiple times do not get multiple jackets, though.
8. D. Plants or trees. The course was once a plant nursery, so each hole is named after the plant or tree it would help grow.
9. A. Tenth. What was once the opening hole, now the tenth, became much tougher when Maxwell moved the green back 50 yards atop a hill.
10. B. 11-13. It was named by Herbert Warren Wind, a sports author who was looking for a way to describe where most of the action took place on the course.
11. C. Jordan Spieth. It was not a great moment, but it did add to the lore of Amen Corner.
12. D. 17th. It was named the Eisenhower Pine because he hit it so often that he proposed that they cut it down. The tree was removed in 2014 after suffering damage from an ice storm.
13. B. Sarazen Bridge. It was dedicated to him in 1955, three years before the Nelson and Hogan Bridges. Rae's Creek is also a named feature on the course.
14. B. Seven. Chairmen are not limited to a specific number of years of service, and they are the only people in the organization allowed to publicly discuss the Masters Tournament.
15. D. 2012. The club extended memberships to Condoleezza Rice and Darla Moore.

16. C. 54. Only the final round is played at Augusta National, while the first two rounds are played at Champions Retreat Golf Club.
17. B. 1949. Sam Snead won the 1949 Masters, which began the tradition of the green jacket.
18. C. Gary Player. He was supposed to bring it back one year after his victory, but he kept coming up with silly excuses. The course eventually let him keep it.

Did You Know?

For decades, Augusta National employed a group of Black men as the staff caddies. It was not until 1982 that players were allowed to use their regular caddies at the Masters.

CHAPTER 28:
Shinnecock Hills Golf Club

1. Shinnecock Hills is located between Peconic Bay and which body of water?

    A. Hudson River
    B. Atlantic Ocean
    C. Lake Erie
    D. Lake Superior

2. In what year was Shinnecock Hills established?

    A. 1890
    B. 1891
    C. 1894
    D. 1898

3. How many times has the course hosted the U.S. Open?

    A. Three
    B. Four
    C. Five
    D. Six

4. When the land was selected to build the course, it was just east of which natural feature?

    A. Shinnecock foothills
    B. Shinnecock Canal
    C. Shinnecock Bay
    D. Shinnecock Woods

5. How many years after the course opened in 1892 did Shinnecock Hills also open a nine-hole ladies' course?

    A. One
    B. Two
    C. 46
    D. 74

6. Which iteration of the U.S. Open did Shinnecock Hills first host?

    A. Inaugural
    B. Second
    C. Fourth
    D. Seventh

7. In which year did Shinnecock expand from 5,000 yards to 6,740 yards?

    A. 1922
    B. 1927
    C. 1929
    D. 1931

8. Though it remained a par-70 course, how many more yards did the course add for the 2018 U.S. Open?

    A. 400
    B. 500
    C. 600
    D. 700

9. What was the lowest score of the four modern U.S. Opens hosted at Shinnecock Hills?

    A. 276
    B. 279
    C. 280
    D. 281

10. How many par-fives does Shinnecock Hills have?

    A. Zero
    B. One
    C. Two
    D. Four

11. What is the name of the longest hole at Shinnecock Hills?

    A. Montauk
    B. Shinnecock
    C. Road Side
    D. Eastward Ho

12. What is the shortest hole at Shinnecock Hills?

    A. Eden
    B. Redan
    C. Home
    D. Hill Head

13. How many par-fours at Shinnecock Hills are longer than 500 yards?

A. Zero
B. One
C. Two
D. Three

14. At the 1977 Walker Cup, played at Shinnecock Hills, the United States destroyed Great Britain and Ireland by what margin?

    A. 16 to eight
    B. 15 to nine
    C. 14 to ten
    D. 13 to 11

15. During the 1986 U.S. Open at Shinnecock Hills, ten players were either leading or tied for the lead throughout the final round. Who came out on top?

    A. Lee Trevino
    B. Raymond Floyd
    C. Hal Sutton
    D. Chip Beck

16. The 100th anniversary of the U.S. Open took place at Shinnecock Hills, but which iteration of the U.S. Open was it?

    A. 93rd
    B. 95th
    C. 97th
    D. 98th

17. Brooks Koepka was only the third player since World War II to defend his U.S. Open title. Besides Koepka's defense in 2018, who did it most recently?

    A. Ben Hogan
    B. Arnold Palmer
    C. Jack Nicklaus
    D. Curtis Strange

18. For the 2018 U.S. Open at Shinnecock Hills, the USGA changed the playoff format from a full round of 18 holes to how many holes of aggregate play?

    A. Two

B. Three
C. Four
D. Five

Chapter 28 Answers:

1. B. Atlantic Ocean. The course is in Southampton on Long Island, in New York.
2. B. 1891. It is believed to be the oldest golf club in the United States. The course was built one year later.
3. C. Five. It is also scheduled to host the tournament again in 2026.
4. B. Shinnecock Canal. Though they bought the original 80 acres, the nearby Shinnecock Indian Nation claims the land was stolen from them.
5. A. One. The ladies' course opened in 1893, making it the first ladies' golf course in the history of the United States.
6. B. Second. Shinnecock Hills has the distinction of hosting the second-ever U.S. Open in 1896, which was only a 36-hole event back then.
7. D. 1931. Architect William Flynn redesigned the course, retaining five of the previous holes and the green of a sixth hole.
8. D. 700. Several new tees were added, but the routing was kept the same.
9. A. 276. Retief Goosen shot -4 on the tournament to win in 2004, two strokes ahead of Phil Mickelson.
10. C. Two. Numbers five and 16 are the only par-fives on the course.
11. B. Shinnecock. As of 2024, Shinnecock is 616 yards from the U.S. Open tees.
12. D. Hill Head. It is 159 yards from the U.S. Open tees, though two of the other par-threes on the course are also under 200 yards.
13. C. Two. Peconic, the third hole, is 500 yards on the dot. Thom's Elbow, the 14th, is 519 yards.
14. A. 16 to eight. It was the only time that Shinnecock Hills hosted the Walker Cup Tournament.
15. B. Raymond Floyd. It was Floyd's only U.S. Open title.
16. B. 95th. Corey Pavin won the only major championship of his career that weekend, two strokes in front of Greg Norman.
17. D. Curtis Strange. He successfully defended his U.S. Open title back in 1989.
18. A. Two. However, playoffs have never been needed at a U.S. Open played at Shinnecock Hills.

Did You Know?

Shinnecock Hills was one of the five founding clubs of the United States Golf Association, which was established in New York City.

CHAPTER 29:
Pebble Beach Golf Links

1. Pebble Beach Golf Links began as part of a resort hotel built by Charles Crocker, who was a baron of what industry?

    A. Railroad
    B. Banking
    C. Mining
    D. Shipping

2. While the hotel was opened in 1880, the golf course was not opened until which year?

    A. 1901
    B. 1913
    C. 1919
    D. 1925

3. Though it had only recently opened, the course underwent an extensive revision in which year?

    A. 1920
    B. 1924
    C. 1925
    D. 1928

4. When was the first Pebble Beach Championship for Women played?

    A. 1917
    B. 1923
    C. 1925
    D. 1930

5. The Monterey Peninsula Open was the first pro tournament at Pebble Beach. How much was the purse for this 1926 tournament?

    A. $2,000
    B. $5,000
    C. $6,500
    D. $7,000

6. Three years later, in 1929, Pebble Beach hosted its first major championship. Which one was it?

    A. PGA Championship
    B. U.S. Open
    C. U.S. Amateur

D. Masters Tournament

7. For 20 years, Pebble Beach played host to which tournament, beginning in 1967?

   A. PGA Championship
   B. U.S. Amateur
   C. California Women's Amateur Championship
   D. California Men's Amateur Championship

8. Beginning in 1947, Pebble Beach played host to the Bing Crosby National Pro-Am tournament. How many times has Pebble Beach hosted the tournament as of 2024?

   A. 73
   B. 52
   C. 44
   D. 19

9. Pebble Beach hosted the Nabisco Championship once, in 1988. Who won that tournament?

   A. Bill Glasson
   B. Tom Purtzer
   C. Mark Calcavecchia
   D. Curtis Strange

10. As of 2025, Pebble Beach has hosted the U.S. Open how many times?

    A. Four
    B. Five
    C. Six
    D. Seven

11. Which player, who went on to win the 1972 U.S. Open at Pebble Beach, hit a one-iron on the par-three 17th that took one bounce and struck the flagstick, leaving a tap-in for birdie?

    A. Arnold Palmer
    B. Jack Nicklaus
    C. Bruce Crampton
    D. Lee Trevino

12. At the 1982 U.S. Open, also on the 17th hole, which player made an incredible chip-in to take the lead from Jack Nicklaus on his way to a major championship victory?

    A. Tom Watson
    B. Bill Rogers
    C. Dan Pohl
    D. Bobby Clampett

13. At the 1992 U.S. Open, how many players finished the difficult tournament with scores under par?

    A. Zero
    B. One
    C. Two
    D. Three

14. Despite the tough conditions at the 1992 U.S. Open at Pebble Beach, Gil Morgan was looking good with what score early on in the third round before he fell back?

    A. -12
    B. -10
    C. -8
    D. -5

15. The 2000 U.S. Open was dominated by which player, who won his first U.S. Open with 15 strokes to spare, a record?

    A. Ernie Else
    B. Miguel Angel Jimenez
    C. Vijay Singh
    D. Tiger Woods

16. Going into the 2000 U.S. Open, the defending champion was not in the field, as he had passed away in an aviation accident. Who was it?

    A. Paul Lawrie
    B. Payne Stewart
    C. Paul Azinger
    D. Phil Mickelson

17. Which player became the first from Northern Ireland to win the U.S. Open in 40 years when he won the 2010 tournament at Pebble Beach?

    A. Ernie Els
    B. Rory McIlroy
    C. Graeme McDowell
    D. Sam Snead

18. Which player broke Brooks Koepka's streak of U.S. Open victories by winning the 2019 tournament at Pebble Beach?

    A. Viktor Hovland
    B. Gary Woodland
    C. Xander Schauffele
    D. Jon Rahm

Chapter 29 Answers:

1. A. Railroad. The resort hotel built by Crocker was named the Hotel del Monte that existed until 1942.
2. C. 1919. It was designed by two champion golfers, Jack Neville and Douglas Grant.
3. D. 1928. H. Chandler Egan made substantial changes to the course, but these would stick around for many decades before the next revamp.
4. B. 1923. Marion Hollins won the event over Doreen Kavanaugh, three years before the course hosted its first pro tournament.
5. B. $5,000. "Lighthorse" Harry Cooper won the tournament with a +5 score.
6. C. U.S. Amateur. Jimmy Johnston of Minnesota won the event, though Bobby Jones did finish first in the stroke play qualifier.
7. C. California Women's Amateur Championship. They hosted the tournament every year until it moved on to another course in 1987.
8. A. 73. Though the tournament uses two different courses every year, Pebble Beach has seen much more play than the next course on the list, Spyglass Hill, with 52 times as host.
9. D. Curtis Strange. It was the Tour Championship of the season, and Strange won the event, the 16th win of his career.
10. C. Six. The course was the host in 1972, 1982, 1992, 2000, 2010, and 2019. It will get its seventh chance to host in 2027.
11. B. Jack Nicklaus. It was his 11th major championship and a shot that has gone down in golf history.
12. A. Tom Watson. He denied Jack Nicklaus a fifth U.S. Open title, and Nicklaus would only win one more major, in 1986.
13. C. Two. Tom Kite won the tournament with a -3, two strokes ahead of Jeff Sluman.
14. A. -12. Two double bogeys and five bogeys in the final round were a big part of that collapse.
15. D. Tiger Woods. Pebble Beach was moved up two years in the rotation of U.S. Open hosts because of the new millennium. The USGA wanted the tournament to be special.
16. B. Payne Stewart. The tournament started with a ceremony the night before on the 18th green of the course.

17. C. Graeme McDowell. He won the tournament, finishing one stroke ahead of Gregory Havret. Ernie Els finished third, while Woods and Mickelson tied for fourth.
18. B. Gary Woodland. Koepka came within four strokes of being the first player in more than 100 years to win three straight U.S. Open titles.

Did You Know?

The Pebble Beach Company has agreed to leave 635 acres of forest undeveloped to help protect many rare and endangered species in the area. This has kept the company from expanding its golf course development in the area.

CHAPTER 30:
Pinehurst No. 2

1. Pinehurst No. 2 is part of Pinehurst Resort. How many 18-hole courses are attributed to Pinehurst Resort?

   A. Two
   B. Four
   C. Seven
   D. Ten

2. Pinehurst No. 2 was completed nine years after the first Pinehurst course. What year was Pinehurst No. 2 completed and opened?

   A. 1902
   B. 1905
   C. 1907
   D. 1909

3. For almost 50 years, Pinehurst was the home of which tournament, considered one of the most prestigious in the United States at the time?

   A. North and South Open
   B. East and West Open
   C. North Carolina Open
   D. United North and South Amateur Championship

4. What was the first PGA Tour major played at Pinehurst?

   A. 1933 U.S. Open
   B. 1936 PGA Championship
   C. 1939 U.S. Open
   D. 1948 PGA Championship

5. After that first major championship, the course would not host another major championship until which year?

   A. 1992
   B. 1995
   C. 1997
   D. 1999

6. Which non-major tournament did Pinehurst host in 1951?

   A. Tour Championship
   B. Walker Cup
   C. Ryder Cup
   D. Presidents Cup

7. When did the U.S. Open return to Pinehurst again after the successful showing in 1999?

    A. 2020
    B. 2015
    C. 2010
    D. 2005

8. Which former golfer helped to renovate Pinehurst No. 2 back in 2011?

    A. Ben Crenshaw
    B. Arnold Palmer
    C. Jack Nicklaus
    D. Tom Watson

9. The U.S. Open returned to Pinehurst again in 2014. Who captured the victory for that major championship?

    A. Erik Compton
    B. Martin Kaymer
    C. Rickie Fowler
    D. Keegan Bradley

10. In an unusual move by the USGA, which tournament was held at Pinehurst No. 2 just one week after the 2014 U.S. Open?

    A. Ryder Cup
    B. Tour Championship
    C. U.S. Women's Open
    D. PGA Championship

11. The 1994 U.S. Senior Open was held at Pinehurst. What was the winner's score?

    A. +2
    B. E
    C. -1
    D. -10

12. Though it is a par-72 course for the blue and white tees, Pinehurst No. 2 becomes a par-70 course for the U.S. Open. Which of these holes becomes a par-four instead of a par-five?

    A. Eight
    B. Ten

C. 14
D. 18

13. What is the longest hole at Pinehurst No. 2?

    A. Five
    B. Ten
    C. 14
    D. 16

14. How long is the longest par-three on Pinehurst No. 2?

    A. 242
    B. 215
    C. 205
    D. 202

15. The 2008 U.S. Amateur took place at Pinehurst No. 2. Danny Lee, from which country, won the event?

    A. United States
    B. New Zealand
    C. England
    D. South Africa

16. After the 2008 U.S. Amateur, how many years later did the event return to Pinehurst No. 2?

    A. 11
    B. 12
    C. 13
    D. 14

17. Where is the statue of Payne Stewart on Pinehurst No. 2?

    A. Near the clubhouse entrance
    B. Beside the tee box on number one
    C. Near the green on 18
    D. Beside the tee box on number ten

18. A partnership with the USGA named Pinehurst the first "anchor site" in which year?

    A. 2020
    B. 2021
    C. 2023
    D. 2024

Chapter 30 Answers:

1. D. Ten. Though there are several nice courses on the resort, Pinehurst No. 2 has established itself as one of the most incredible courses in the world.
2. C. 1907. Architect Donald Ross himself said it was "the fairest test of championship golf I have ever designed."
3. A. North and South Open. It still hosts the annual North and South Amateur Golf Championships to this day, running strong since 1901.
4. B. 1936 PGA Championship. The tournament was won by Denny Shute, who defeated Jimmy Thomson three and two in the final.
5. D. 1999. The U.S. Open came to town that year, and Payne Stewart claimed the title.
6. C. Ryder Cup. The United States team won easily, 9.5 to 2.5.
7. D. 2005. It was another great event, and New Zealand's Michael Campbell went home with the title.
8. A. Ben Crenshaw. The goal of the renovation was to restore the course to its original design, as Donald Ross had intended.
9. B. Martin Kaymer. It was a dominant tournament for the German player, who had eight strokes to spare after making his final putt.
10. C. U.S. Women's Open. Michelle Wie won the tournament with the only score under par, at -2.
11. D. -10 . Simon Hobday finished one stroke ahead of Jim Albus and Graham Marsh.
12. A. Eight. The hole plays 502 yards for the pros, which is a very long par-four.
13. B. Ten. The par-five tenth hole is 617 yards from tee to green, the longest on the course.
14. A. 242. The par-three sixth hole is very long, and it doesn't help that the green is surrounded by bunkers.
15. B. New Zealand. Lee turned pro one year later and also joined LIV golf.
16. A. 11. Pinehurst No. 2 hosted the 2019 U.S. Amateur, where Andy Ogletree won the event.
17. C. Near the green on 18. Stewart's statue shows him celebrating his final putt at the 1999 U.S. Open, which he won before his passing.
18. A. 2020. It was the beginning of the first extended partnership between a course and the USGA.

Did You Know?

Pinehurst No. 2 was ranked as the sixth-best public golf course in the United States according to the 2019–2020 *Golf Digest* course rankings.

CHAPTER 31:
Royal County Down Golf Club

1. In what year was Royal County Down Golf Club established?

    A. 1881
    B. 1886
    C. 1889
    D. 1891

2. Once the first nine holes were completed and opened to play, who did the club council pay to come and advise on how to construct a back nine?

    A. Old Tom Morris
    B. Young Tom Morris
    C. Willie Park Sr.
    D. Harry Vardon

3. After opening the first nine holes in March of 1889, how quickly did they expand to 18 holes?

    A. One year
    B. Ten years
    C. 18 months
    D. Three years

4. Who served as the Captain of the club in 1898, then as the "Convenor of the Green" from 1900 to 1913?

    A. Ben Sayers
    B. Harry Vardon
    C. George Combe
    D. J.H. Taylor

5. Harry Colt was asked how the course could be improved, so he started working on it in which year?

    A. 1920
    B. 1925
    C. 1930
    D. 1935

6. Architect Donald Steel strengthened which two holes in 1997, upping the challenge even further?

    A. One and two
    B. Nine and ten

C. 12 and 13
D. 17 and 18

7. In 1893, Royal County Down hosted the Irish Open Amateur Championship. How many times had the tournament taken place before the 1893 iteration?

    A. Zero
    B. One
    C. Two
    D. Three

8. In 1899, the course hosted the British Ladies Amateur Golf Championship for the first time. Who won the tournament that year?

    A. May Hezlet
    B. Jessie Magill
    C. Lena Thomson
    D. Elinor Nevile

9. In 1963, Brigitte Varangot of which country won The Women's Amateur Championship at Royal County Down?

    A. England
    B. United States
    C. France
    D. Germany

10. Belen Mozo defeated Anna Nordqvist of which country to win the 2006 Women's Amateur at Royal County Down?

    A. Sweden
    B. Finland
    C. Spain
    D. Ireland

11. Most recently, Emily Toy defeated Amelia Garvey one up to win the Women's Amateur at Royal County Down during which year?

    A. 2017
    B. 2019
    C. 2022
    D. 2024

12. In 2012, Europe defeated the United States at Royal County Down in a Cup named for which golfer?

    A. Jack Nicklaus
    B. Byron Nelson
    C. Arnold Palmer
    D. Ben Hogan

13. In 1968, at Royal County Down, the United States defeated Great Britain and Ireland in the Curtis Cup by what margin?

    A. 10.5 to 7.5
    B. 11.5 to 6.5
    C. 13 to 5
    D. 12 to 6

14. The 2015 Irish Open, a tournament that is part of the European Tour, took place at Royal County Down. Soren Kjeldsen tied with two other players at what score before defeating them in a playoff?

    A. E
    B. -1
    C. -2
    D. -3

15. The 2007 Walker Cup was closely contested, with the USA coming out ahead by how many points?

    A. 0.5
    B. 1
    C. 1.5
    D. 2

16. Rasmus Hojgaard won the 2024 Irish Open at Royal County Down, finishing one stroke ahead of which player?

    A. Ryan Fox
    B. Rory McIlroy
    C. Hurly Long
    D. Vincent Norman

17. Which is the longest hole at Royal County Down Golf Club?

    A. One
    B. 12
    C. 15

D. 18

18. The shortest par-three on the course can be found on which hole?

    A. Four
    B. Seven
    C. Ten
    D. 14

Chapter 31 Answers:

1. C. 1889. A group of businessmen from Belfast didn't know what they were giving birth to, but history was made that year.
2. A. Old Tom Morris. The group made sure they did not pay Morris more than £4 for his information and help. Still, the low price got results for the golf course.
3. A. One year. By the spring of 1890, the course was a full 18 holes thanks to Morris' guidance.
4. C. George Combe. Combe contributed to alterations on the course during his time as Convenor, but several other great golfers visited to give their advice.
5. B. 1925. Colt's adjustments led to the creation of the current fourth and ninth holes, two of the most beautiful golf holes in the world.
6. D. 17 and 18. The 18th hole became one of the most difficult finishing holes in the world after Steel's adjustments.
7. B. One. Royal County Down had the honor of hosting the second iteration of the tournament, which had been played at Royal Portrush the year before.
8. A. May Hezlet. She defeated Jessie Magill two and one to capture the championship.
9. C. France. She defeated Philomena Garvey of Ireland three and one to take the title.
10. A. Sweden. Mozo won the match three and one to capture the crown.
11. B. 2019. Toy went on to turn professional in 2022.
12. C. Arnold Palmer. The Arnold Palmer Cup is a competition between teams of college/university golfers.
13. A. 10.5 to 7.5. The competition between amateur women golfers is held every other year.
14. C. -2. He defeated Eddie Pepperell and Bernd Wiesberger to capture the victory.
15. B. 1. It was a star-studded event, with Rory McIlroy and Dustin Johnson headlining their respective teams.
16. B. Rory McIlroy. Hojgaard shot -9 for the tournament to take the victory.
17. D. 18. The par-five 18th hole is 548 yards from the tips, just nine more yards than the first hole of the course.

18. B. Seven. The seventh hole is only 144 yards from the tips. Not every hole is a monster.

Did You Know?

In 2024, *Golf Digest* ranked Royal County Down Golf Club as the World's Greatest Course.

CHAPTER 32:
Muirfield

1. Muirfield overlooks which water feature in East Lothian, Scotland?

    A. Firth of Forth
    B. Firth of Clyde
    C. Solway Firth
    D. Cromarty Firth

2. The Honorable Company of Edinburgh Golfers was founded in what year, well before they called Muirfield their home?

    A. 1739
    B. 1744
    C. 1790
    D. 1811

3. The HCEG moved from Leith Links to Musselburgh Old Course in what year, looking for a less crowded place to play?

    A. 1827
    B. 1830
    C. 1833
    D. 1836

4. When the group built their new private course at Muirfield in 1891, they took what with them?

    A. The Amateur
    B. The Open Championship
    C. The Women's Amateur
    D. The Team Amateur

5. In 1892, Muirfield hosted the Open Championship for the first time. It was also the first time the tournament was played over how many holes?

    A. 36
    B. 54
    C. 63
    D. 72

6. Women were barred from membership at Muirfield until what year?

    A. 1933
    B. 1989
    C. 2000
    D. 2017

7. Since the Open Championship in 1959 and concluding at the most recent Open in 2013, how many yards have been added to Muirfield to make it more challenging?

    A. 192
    B. 194
    C. 386
    D. 451

8. Of all the Open Championship winners at Muirfield over the years, which player shot the lowest aggregate score?

    A. Phil Mickelson
    B. Tom Watson
    C. Nick Faldo
    D. Ernie Els

9. James Braid won two consecutive Open Championships hosted by Muirfield in 1901 and 1906. Who is the only other golfer to accomplish that feat?

    A. Phil Mickelson
    B. Tom Watson
    C. Nick Faldo
    D. Ernie Els

10. Walter Hagen won the 1929 Open Championship, but what was his score for the tournament?

    A. -1
    B. E
    C. +4
    D. +12

11. The Senior British Open has only been played at Muirfield once. When was that?

    A. 2007
    B. 2009
    C. 2013
    D. 2019

12. The Women's British Open has also only been played at Muirfield once. Who won that tournament in 2022?

- A. Chun In-gee
- B. Ashleigh Buhai
- C. Hinako Shibuno
- D. Minjee Lee

13. Muirfield decided to change one of its holes from a par-five to a par-four for the 1966 Open Championship. Which hole was changed?

    - A. 14
    - B. 15
    - C. 17
    - D. 18

14. Which of these players never won an Open Championship at Muirfield?

    - A. Tiger Woods
    - B. Phil Mickelson
    - C. Gary Player
    - D. Lee Trevino

15. Walter Hagen won £100 for his 1929 victory at the Open Championship in Muirfield. How many pounds did Phil Mickelson win in 2013?

    - A. £125,000
    - B. £440,000
    - C. £720,000
    - D. £945,000

16. What is the longest hole at Muirfield?

    - A. Five
    - B. Nine
    - C. 17
    - D. 18

17. Which of these holes at Muirfield is the shortest?

    - A. Four
    - B. Seven
    - C. 13
    - D. 16

18. Muirfield has hosted the Open Championship 16 times. Which of these courses has hosted the tournament more than that?
    A. Prestwick
    B. Royal Troon
    C. Carnoustie
    D. Turnberry

Chapter 32 Answers:

1. A. Firth of Forth. It is the estuary of several Scottish rivers, and the River Forth is one of them.
2. B. 1744. The group is famous for producing some of the first rules associated with the game of golf.
3. D. 1836. The HCEG was not going to be happy here, either, so they would eventually decide to build their own course.
4. B. The Open Championship. Musselburgh and its members were not pleased with that development, but history could not be stopped.
5. D. 72. It was the first time in the history of golf that a tournament lasted that long.
6. D. 2017. The club reacted when the R&A removed Muirfield from the rotation of Open Championship courses. Only then did women get the chance to become members.
7. C. 386. In 1959, the course was 6,806 yards and par-72. In 2013, it was 7,192 yards and par-71.
8. B. Tom Watson. He shot 271 in 1980, one shot better than Nick Faldo's 272 in 1992.
9. C. Nick Faldo. He won the tournament in 1987, then again in 1992, the next time it was hosted by Muirfield.
10. D. +12. He shot 75 in the first, third, and fourth rounds. A second-round 67 was good enough to keep him atop the leaderboard.
11. A. 2007. Tom Watson won that tournament with an even score.
12. B. Ashleigh Buhai. She defeated Chun In-gee in a sudden-death playoff to capture the major championship.
13. A. 14. The 462-yard hole was made more difficult by making it a par-four.
14. A. Tiger Woods. The only ones Tiger would have played in, the 2002 and 2013 tournaments, were won by Ernie Els and Phil Mickelson.
15. D. £945,000. Mickelson shot a 66 in the final round for a total of -3 on the tournament.
16. C. 17. The par-five 17th hole is 578 yards long, 20 yards longer than the par-five ninth hole.
17. B. Seven. The par-three seventh hole is 187 yards, only one yard shorter than the par-three 16th hole.
18. A. Prestwick. Since the first Open Championship in 1860, it has hosted the tournament 24 times.

Did You Know?

Old Tom Morris helped in the original design of Muirfield, though he never had a chance to compete for an Open Championship there.

CHAPTER 33:
Carnoustie Golf Links

1. Historically, which century has evidence of golf being played at Carnoustie?

    A. 13th
    B. 14th
    C. 15th
    D. 16th

2. What year did the official Carnoustie Golf Links course open?

    A. 1824
    B. 1842
    C. 1869
    D. 1896

3. How many holes did the original Carnoustie Golf Links have?

    A. Seven
    B. Nine
    C. Ten
    D. 18

4. Old Tom Morris extended the course to 18 holes in what year?

    A. 1854
    B. 1859
    C. 1866
    D. 1867

5. After James Braid made more modifications in 1926, Carnoustie hosted the Open Championship in what year?

    A. 1928
    B. 1929
    C. 1930
    D. 1931

6. How many times has Carnoustie hosted The Amateur Championship, the oldest amateur event in the world?

    A. Zero
    B. One
    C. Three
    D. Four

7. Which golfer infamously collapsed under pressure at the 1999 Open Championship?

    A. Jean Van de Velde
    B. Justin Leonard
    C. Angel Cabrera
    D. Greg Norman

8. Which player needed a four-hole playoff to overcome Sergio Garcia and win the 2007 Open Championship at Carnoustie?

    A. Andres Romero
    B. Padraig Harrington
    C. Ernie Els
    D. Stewart Cink

9. In 2018, Tiger Woods and Rory McIlroy couldn't catch which player, who went on to win the Open Championship at Carnoustie?

    A. Justin Rose
    B. Xander Schauffele
    C. Francesco Molinari
    D. Kevin Kisner

10. The third hole of the course is called Jockie's Burn for the hazard on the hole. Where is it?

    A. Middle of fairway
    B. Right of fairway
    C. Front of green
    D. Right of green

11. In September 2003, which hole was renamed Hogan's Alley after Ben Hogan's daring tactics in the 1953 Open Championship?

    A. Three
    B. Four
    C. Five
    D. Six

12. The 14th hole is called "Spectacles" because of what in the middle of the fairway?

    A. Ponds
    B. Cart paths
    C. Bunkers

D. Trees

13. Hole 17 has what name, as one section of the fairway is separated from the rest?

    A. Barry's Burn
    B. Home
    C. Southward Ho
    D. Island

14. What is the name of the longest par-four at Carnoustie?

    A. Hogan's Alley
    B. Spectacles
    C. Home
    D. Southward Ho

15. What is the name of the shortest hole at Carnoustie?

    A. Short
    B. Whins
    C. Lucky Slap
    D. Barry Burn

16. How many par-threes are at Carnoustie Golf Links?

    A. Two
    B. Three
    C. Four
    D. Five

17. What is the course record at Carnoustie?

    A. 63
    B. 62
    C. 61
    D. 60

18. The Senior Open Championship has been played at Carnoustie three times. Who won it in 2024?

    A. Richard Green
    B. Paul Broadhurst
    C. K.J. Choi
    D. Stephen Ames

Chapter 33 Answers:

1. D. 16th. Though golf looked much different back then, it was still a part of the location going forward in time.
2. B. 1842. Old Tom Morris and Allan Robertson teamed up to design the course.
3. C. Ten. Those ten holes crossed the Barry Burn more than once, causing players trouble.
4. D. 1867. A new railway brought more golfers to the course, which led to the expansion.
5. D. 1931. Tommy Armour of Edinburgh won that tournament with an aggregate score of 296.
6. D. Four. It first hosted the event in 1947, and most recently in 1992.
7. A. Jean Van de Velde. He had a three-stroke lead on the final hole of the tournament. He triple bogeyed the hole and then lost to Paul Lawrie in a playoff.
8. B. Padraig Harrington. Both players shot -7 on the tournament to reach the playoff.
9. C. Francesco Molinari. His -8 for the tournament was two shots better than four players who tied for second place.
10. C. Front of green. Any ball that is not hit far enough will be in trouble thanks to the small stream of water running across the approach to the green.
11. D. Six. Hogan dared to aim for the space between the bunkers and the out-of-bounds fencing. Paul Lawrie, 1999 Open Champion, named the hole after Hogan.
12. C. Bunkers. They're called spectacles because they look like peeping eyes from a distance.
13. D. Island. Players have to be confident in their distance to make sure it lands safely away from the water.
14. D. Southward Ho. It is 504 yards long, just six yards shorter than the par-five Spectacles.
15. B. Whins. It is 171 yards long, and Short is 183 yards (because, of course, you wanted to know).
16. B. Three. Most standard courses have four or more of them, but Carnoustie does not.
17. A. 63. Tommy Fleetwood shot 63 in 2017.
18. C. K.J. Choi. He shot -10 on the tournament and finished two strokes ahead of Richard Green.

Did You Know?

Carnoustie has two more courses on its property, though they are not as prestigious as the Golf Links.

CHAPTER 34:
Unbeatable Records

1. Only two golfers have won a PGA Tour event seven times or more. Which of these is one of them?

    A. Sam Snead
    B. Harry Vardon
    C. Jack Nicklaus
    D. James Braid

2. Which player has 12 Champions Tour major championships, three more than the next player on the list?

    A. Gary Player
    B. Bernhard Langer
    C. Jack Nicklaus
    D. Hale Irwin

3. There have been 18 recorded double eagles, or albatrosses, at major championships. As of 2024, who has scored one most recently?

    A. Paul Lawrie
    B. Shaun Micheel
    C. Louis Oosthuizen
    D. Nick Watney

4. Only one player completed the original Grand Slam. Who was it?

    A. Gene Sarazen
    B. Tommy Armour
    C. Bobby Jones
    D. Old Tom Morris

5. How many players have completed the Career Modern Grand Slam?

    A. Five
    B. Six
    C. Seven
    D. Eight

6. Who sits atop the list for most major championship victories?

    A. Gary Player
    B. Ben Hogan
    C. Tiger Woods
    D. Jack Nicklaus

7. Woods and Nicklaus both had the majority of their major victories at which major?

    A. U.S. Open
    B. British Open
    C. PGA Championship
    D. Masters

8. How many LPGA players have completed a career Grand Slam?

    A. Six
    B. Seven
    C. Eight
    D. Nine

9. Patty Berg sits atop the list of LPGA major championship wins with how many?

    A. 13
    B. 14
    C. 15
    D. 16

10. After Harry Vardon (who won The Open six times before 1914), how many players have won The Open five times?

    A. One
    B. Two
    C. Three
    D. Four

11. There are four players with four wins at the U.S. Open. Which of them won it most recently?

    A. Jack Nicklaus
    B. Bobby Jones
    C. Ben Hogan
    D. Willie Anderson

12. Two players have won the PGA Championship five times, and one of them is Jack Nicklaus. Who is the other?

    A. Tiger Woods
    B. Walter Hagen
    C. Gene Sarazen
    D. Brooks Koepka

13. Four players have shot a 58 in professional golf. Who is the only one that did it on the PGA Tour?

    A. Ryo Ishikawa
    B. Kim Seong-hyeon
    C. Jim Furyk
    D. Bryson DeChambeau

14. How many players have shot a -13 for a 59 on their professional round?

    A. Four
    B. Five
    C. Six
    D. Seven

15. Eight amateur players have won a PGA Tour tournament. Who did it in 2024?

    A. Scott Verplank
    B. Frank Stranahan
    C. Fred Haas
    D. Nick Dunlap

16. Who once won 11 PGA Tour events in a row?

    A. Byron Nelson
    B. Tiger Woods
    C. Ben Hogan
    D. Jack Burke Jr.

17. How many PGA tour players have ever put together a streak of four straight wins?

    A. Three
    B. Four
    C. Five
    D. Six

18. Three players have won more than ten games in a single PGA Tour season. Who had the most?

    A. Ben Hogan
    B. Sam Snead
    C. Byron Nelson
    D. Paul Runyan

Chapter 34 Answers:

1. A. Sam Snead. He won the Greater Greensboro Open eight times. Tiger Woods won two different tournaments eight times and another two different tournaments seven times each.
2. B. Bernhard Langer. Included in those 12 are four wins at the Senior Open Championship.
3. D. Nick Watney. He scored one at the 2012 U.S. Open in the first round, on the par-five 17th.
4. C. Bobby Jones. He won all four majors, U.S. and British Amateurs, and U.S. and British Opens, in 1930.
5. A. Five. Jack Nicklaus, Tiger Woods, Ben Hogan, Gary Player, and Gene Sarazen.
6. D. Jack Nicklaus. His total of 18 majors is three ahead of Tiger Woods.
7. D. Masters. Nicklaus won six times at Augusta, and Woods won there five times.
8. B. Seven. Karrie Webb, Mickey Wright, Louise Suggs, Juli Inkster, Pat Bradley, Annika Sorenstam, and Inbee Park.
9. C. 15. She won seven Titleholders Championships and seven Women's Western Opens to go with her one U.S. Women's Open.
10. D. Four. Tom Watson, James Braid, John Henry Taylor, and Peter Thomson.
11. A. Jack Nicklaus. His last win at the U.S. Open was in 1986.
12. B. Walter Hagen. Woods won it four times; Sarazen, Koepka, and Snead each have three.
13. C. Jim Furyk. He shot it in 2016 at the Travelers Championship.
14. D. Seven. Casey Jarvis of the Sunshine Tour in South Africa did it most recently, in 2023.
15. D. Nick Dunlap. He did it at The American Express in California.
16. A. Byron Nelson. All of those wins came in 1945.
17. B. Four. Byron Nelson (11), Tiger Woods (seven), Ben Hogan (six), and Jack Burke Jr. (four).
18. C. Byron Nelson. He won 18 times in 1945. Hogan did it twice in 1946 and 1948.

Did You Know?

Tiger Woods had winning streaks of seven, six, and five, giving him three of the five highest streaks in golf history.

CONCLUSION

There you have it! The final putt has dropped into the cup, the scorecards are being checked and signed, and players are packing up to go home as the sun sets on the course. This book has so much packed into it!

From players to courses, the biggest moments, and the best records, this book is brimming with the history of the game of golf. Today's game may seem flashy and sleek, but it wasn't always that way. It's important to know how golf has grown, how the game was played in the past, and how it can be remembered and respected.

If there is something new you learned in this book, don't let it stop here! Research these stories and moments deeper so you can learn the great lore that surrounds this game.

Whether it was Old Tom Morris, Byron Nelson, Bobby Jones, Tony Jacklin, or any of the names that are more familiar in the past 50 years, there is plenty more to find out about.

Also, consider passing this book on to someone you know who loves the game of golf. Golf is a beautiful game that is special to play and discuss with others.

For now, say goodbye to the golf course — and know that the sun will rise tomorrow and the dew will cover the grass and wait for you to tee off again. Farewell!

www.ingramcontent.com/pod-product-compliance
Lightning Source LLC
Chambersburg PA
CBHW060947050426
42337CB00052B/1623